upside down

JOY

AN INVERTED LOOK AT SIN, SICKNESS, STRUGGLE, & DEATH

ANDREW MANN

NEW HOPE®
PUBLISHERS
Gospel-Centered. Missions-Driven.

BIRMINGHAM, ALABAMA

New Hope® Publishers
P.O. Box 12065
Birmingham, AL 35202-2065
NewHopePublishers.com
New Hope Publishers is a division of WMU®.

Library of Congress Cataloging-in-Publication Data

Mann, Andrew, 1982-
  Upside-down joy : an inverted look at sin, sickness, struggle, and death / Andrew Mann.
    pages cm
  ISBN 978-1-59669-440-8 (sc)
  1. Mann, Andrew, 1982- 2. Christian biography--New York. 3. Joy--Religious aspects--Christianity. 4. Suffering--Religious aspects--Christianity. I. Title.
  BR1725.M263A3 2015
  267'.186092--dc23
  [B]
                    2015018692

Product team: Tina Atchenson, Mark Bethea, Joyce Dinkins, Melissa Hall, Reagan Jackson, Glynese Northam, Maegan Roper, Jade Stewart

ISBN-10: 1-59669-440-8
ISBN-13: 978-1-59669-440-8

N154118 • 0915 • 3M

ACKNOWLEDGMENTS

With thanks to the many characters whose lives and stories have influenced mine.

"Now to Him who is able to do above and beyond all that we ask or think according to the power that works in us—to Him be glory in the church and in Christ Jesus to all generations, forever and ever. Amen." (EPHESIANS 3:20–21)

CONTENTS

SIN

SICKNESS

FOREWORD

"These men who have turned the world upside down have come here too" (ACTS 17:6).

Get ready to have your heart turned upside down. This story is a twisting journey on the inside and a twisting journey on the outside.

The ancients used to say, "A good speaker is simply a good person who speaks well." Good speaking alone is not enough. By the same token, in one sense, a good writer is simply a good person who writes well. For me, in good writing, the integrity of the person burns through. Andrew Mann is one of those writers.

He has integrity as a person. I have known Andrew since he was a freshman in college, and his trajectory has been remarkable. From the college experience to working with troubled children and teens in Manhattan, in Chicago, and ultimately in a challenging area of the South Bronx—I have watched him develop. One leader told me later he never thought Andrew would make it. Andrew did. Graffiti 2 and Andrew along with his famous therapy dog, Proof, became a story for the nation. An unusual church was born, an upside-down church, which proved to be a place for those who sometimes didn't even realize they were looking for a home.

Andrew combines a tender heart for God with an iron resolve. I have been a pastor of a church and community ministry for almost 30 years, and I have heard many people come to the city and share big dreams. That is nothing new. The question I am asking as I listen is whether the size of the commitment matches the size of the dream. For Andrew, it does.

When Andrew received his cancer diagnosis, he found a way to turn that upside down, telling others about his "cancerous joy." He let the experience bring him closer to God rather than drive him away, with a strong sense of humor, openness, and resolve. When I think of this, sometimes it still makes me put my hand to my mouth in wonder.

Andrew has integrity as a person, but you will also find that Andrew is a good writer. Along with sharing his own outward journey as a pastor in one of the most difficult neighborhoods in the nation, he shares his internal journey. Perhaps every story is in some ways a story about our search for a father—coming to terms with the father who is there or who is absent, who is kind or who is abusive, who understands or who doesn't. As you read about Andrew's journey with his own father, you may not realize what I see. I see the number of young people for whom Andrew has served as a father, a silent center of gravity for many in a world that seems to be spinning out of control. Andrew has been a father to the fatherless, and he writes about it in his own distinctive way.

So through the laughter and the heartbreak of Andrew's story, get ready to be turned upside down. Andrew is too modest to share with you the number of people he has affected. I hope you will be one of them. Perhaps the same thing will happen to you that happened to me as I read the book. By being turned upside down, I realized that I was really coming right side up.

Dr. Taylor Field

PASTOR, DIRECTOR
Graffiti Community Ministries
New York City

INTRODUCTION

Life is a story. The story isn't about me. It's a grander story, an eternal one. There is an Author. There are ups and downs. As a character in the story, there have been moments in my story that seem upside down.

AUGUST 18, 2011

"Dad is in a mood. I still get so frustrated with him. It is hard to ignore. I don't know what to do to make the situation better."

DECEMBER 19, 2011

"Andrew, something happened . . . Your dad passed away."

AUGUST 27, 2012

"We found a mass. It looks like testicular cancer."

JULY 27, 2014

"For 16 years of my life, I have been disobedient. I need to be right before God and before my church. I need to be baptized."

However, from where I sit now, retelling my story, I see it all differently. I have learned to see right side up by being turned upside down. God has used the upside-down circumstances of life to give me joy, and He is working to make my joy complete!

By being turned upside down, the upside has come down.

CHAPTER

MY STORY—
THE SIN CHAPTER

JULY 27, 2014

> *"For 16 years of my life, I have been disobedient. I need to be right before God and before my church. I need to be baptized."*

I said these words to the associate pastor of the church I pastor in the Bronx during my own invitation after preaching from John 21. One thought consumed my mind: *Nothing matters more than being obedient to Jesus.* That's not how I've always thought.

As a kid, my life was focused on three areas: family, church, and school. Of course, in small-town life, these three things often intersect.

I was blessed to be raised in a churchgoing family. My dad had faithfully served others in churches throughout his life. In his younger days, he led music in small-town churches across Missouri. After he and my mom married and served several years in the military, they settled down together in the Missouri town where I grew up. Together they committed to a church home and served there faithfully. By the time of my birth, my dad was a deacon and my mom was a nursery worker in the church. There probably was not a child in the congregation whose diaper she hadn't changed!

Church, for me, was an epicenter of activity and relationships. I stayed busy participating in all the programs my church offered. I sang in the choirs and played leading roles in the children's musicals—the boy king Josiah and an Olympic athlete named Hans Bronson.

Having lost my two front teeth when I was three years old, at Christmastime I would travel with my mom's missions group to nursing homes and sing, "All I Want for Christmas Is My Two Front Teeth." With a buzz-cut hairstyle and a smile that showed the genuineness of my song, I would wish them a "Merry Cwith-Mith!"

My church wasn't just a place of activity; it was the source of nearly all the significant relationships of my young life. My friends and my parents' friends were there. We not only socialized at church, but we gathered at one another's houses to enjoy time together. Some of my fondest memories of childhood were the fish fries held at our home by my parents' Sunday School class. On mild summer nights, croquet in the yard was followed by homemade ice cream and a thrilling game of hide-and-seek we called Ghost in the Graveyard. These people invested in my life, and I thank God for them.

In school, I always felt driven to be the best, and I was willing to work hard at it. Early in my childhood, a speech impediment emerged. Sh-, ch-, and especially r- sounds were hard for me to say. Surgically clipping my tongue didn't improve my speech, so my mom asked my elementary school principal if I should be tutored. I remember the conversation because I was standing next to her waiting in line for a meal at our church.

Around that time, our dachshund named Skipper had been neutered. In my innocent boyhood mind, I pieced together all the information I heard and misheard. That evening with a look of concern in my eye and panic in my stomach, I asked my mom, "Are you going to neuter me?"

I wasn't neutered, but I was tutored!

The tutoring helped. Speech therapy over the course of six years fixed the impediment. During those same years, I worked equally hard in school, in sports, in church, and in piano lessons. By sixth grade I was already determined to be the valedictorian of my high school graduating class, something I successfully achieved.

Spending so much time at church, I learned the Bible stories, memorized the verses, and always knew the right thing to say. I knew a person was supposed to be saved and get baptized, so at about age eight, I did just that. Responding to a pastor's invitation, I repeated a prayer and later got baptized.

I knew what a Christian was supposed to do, so it wasn't hard for me to manufacture a Christian life. As a teenager, I played percussion with worship teams, publicly proclaimed Christ at school, served in leadership roles in all the Christian clubs, and was even placed on the pastoral search committee of my church after the pastor of more than 30 years retired.

During my early teen years, I began to realize the hypocrisy of my life. I was a master of religion, yet my faith was insincere. My salvation wasn't based on Jesus; it was based on me. All of my works were little more than religious acts, attempts to please and satisfy both others and myself. The inside was different from the outside.

At age 15 or 16, while at another church, an evangelist's words penetrated my polished and pristine exterior and went straight to my core.

With fire and conviction he said, "God is knocking at the door of your heart, but He doesn't have to keep knocking." I knew I needed to be saved.

I laid across the hardwood floor of my bedroom that night, acknowledging my sin, confessing my need for a savior, and knowing that Jesus was that Savior.

Certainly no one needed to tell me what should come next. I knew I should be baptized. I knew the profession of my faith publicly through baptism was a command of Jesus. However, the fear of losing others' respect clouded my mind.

One thought guided all of my decisions: *What will people think?*

My whole life I took great pleasure from the praises and accolades others had given me because of my Christian life. I had made an idol of myself. Others' respect fueled my behavior.

Therefore, I never got baptized.

I justified this choice thinking, *Everyone knows I'm a Christian. I'm not hiding my faith.*

But no one ever heard me say what I knew inside, that I was a sinner in need of saving, and that Jesus is that Savior.

The Bible warns us that we have an adversary. His name is Satan. Satan wants us to focus on our worldly existence rather than our eternal one. I don't think it really matters to him whether we worship him. He just doesn't want us to worship God.

Furthermore, Satan knows how to use the cracks in our lives to accomplish his goal. He drives in a wedge and slowly wiggles it back and forth, deepening the divide between us and our Creator. For me, that crack was self-worship, and the wedge was doubt.

A memory from my college years is seared in my mind. One night, as I was lying on the top bunk in my dorm room on the Christian college campus I attended in the suburbs of Chicago, listening to 780 WBBM, the wedge of doubt was wiggling back and forth. From this fog emerged a vision that played across the film reel of my mind. This vision was set in the future—I was a pastor, and I was getting baptized. The vision seemed so unlikely because I couldn't escape the thought, *What will people think?*

Satan isn't the only one who uses the cracks in our lives. God was using the cracks in my life as well. The same cracks Satan used to accuse me, God was using to break me, to show me the sin in my life. Awareness of my sin didn't land like a bombshell, but instead slowly crept like a crack across a windshield.

This crack was shattering the idol I had made of myself.

By the summer of 2014, I had been a missionary and pastor of a ministry center and church in the South Bronx for almost ten years. During those years, we had rented several spaces around the neighborhood, including a century-old Jewish synagogue. The synagogue sits on a street with a park on one end and an old Methodist church building on the other. Troubling stories abound about the harsh life on this street. Bullet holes on the facade of our building testify to the stories' legitimacy.

One evening in the basement of this building, surrounded by the frenetic activity of a community meal, a boy tapped me on the back and with tears in his eyes said, "Andrew, I need to be saved." I knew this boy well. Like me he had spent his whole life in church. He had walked the aisle, been baptized, and was respected by everyone around him.

Later that evening I sat with him in the parking lot, and he prayed a prayer of faith in Jesus, making him a new child of God. Moments after opening his eyes, he said, "I need to be baptized." Those words hit me in the face like cold water.

The next morning I was confronted, once again, with a thought that I had so frequently minimized, ignored, and rationalized away.

Andrew, you're saved, but your thinking hasn't changed.

I prayed to God, "Change the way I think. Don't let this leave my mind until I get right before You and right before my church."

I struggled for two weeks. My adversary hammered his wedges. Finally, knowing nothing was more important than obedience to Jesus, I confessed my disobedience and my faith to my friend and associate pastor. That same evening, I did the same in front of my spiritual counselor who is also my friend and mentor.

My idol of self wasn't smashed all at once. For me it took 16 years of cracks inching their way across the veneer of my life. The sincerity and authenticity of this boy in my church poked the glass. The windshield broke. The idol fell and shattered.

On August 3, 2014, as a missionary and pastor, I admitted my sin before my church, repented of that sin, and was baptized.

I didn't care what anyone thought except my Lord and Savior, Jesus.

I went from being a master of religion, concerned about what others thought, to being obedient to Jesus. I only cared what He thought!

2 MY STORY— THE SICKNESS CHAPTER

AUGUST 27, 2012

"We found a mass. It looks like testicular cancer."

Six months before being diagnosed with testicular cancer, I cele-brated my thirtieth birthday. In jest, one of my co-workers at our ministry center in the Bronx unknowingly foreshadowed, "Your body starts falling apart at 30."

While visiting family in Missouri, I figured I should get a checkup. Except for a knee injury, I hadn't been to the doctor for at least 15 years. Catching up with a doctor-friend over lunch, I arranged an appointment for a physical exam.

The next morning I arrived early before his other appointments were scheduled. Blood work was followed by routine health questions. Examining my body, he commented on an enlarged testicle. "It may be nothing, could be a hydrocele, or possibly cancer. We'll need to do an ultrasound to find out."

Taking the elevator to the bottom floor of the clinic, I sat in the radiology waiting room, filled out some paper work, and waited for my name to be called. As I sat, I processed different scenarios.

I wasn't too concerned.

Moments later I lay across a cold table, pants around my legs, with a towel over my waist. The awkward exam began with a cold, jellylike substance followed by the technician doing his work. It wasn't long before he said, "Take a seat in the waiting room. I need to go get the radiologist."

My concern rose a little.

As I sat in the waiting room, blankly staring at the television, the person in the chair next to me couldn't hear the thoughts that fell like raindrops in my stormy mind. *What did he see? What's next? How will I tell my family, my mother? How will this affect my work? I've got so many things to do when I return to New York.*

The door next to me opened. My thoughts subsided as a tall radiologist with glasses stepped out. He took me to a dark room lit only by the light of x-ray lamps and told me, "We found a mass. It looks like testicular cancer."

Returning to my doctor-friend, we talked treatment options and concluded I would return to New York City for treatment.

That was Monday.

My flight back to New York was scheduled for early Wednesday morning. On Tuesday I drove to St. Louis with my mom so we could spend the night in a hotel close to the airport. Throughout the three-hour drive I made phone calls to urology clinics in New York. The earliest available appointment was three weeks away.

While eating a Blizzard from Dairy Queen, a regular stop for me when traveling to or from St. Louis, my phone rang. It was my doctor-friend.

"I talked with an urologist in St. Louis. He said for you to give him a call."

He gave me the urologist's cell phone number.

Moments later I listened to the urologist as he said, "There's a phrase in urology: *Never let the sun go down on testicular cancer . . .* I can see you tomorrow if you want to come in."

The next morning I was in the urologist's office. Like a teacher who had taught the same material for many years, he taught me about testicular cancer. Although rare, it is the most common cancer for males between the ages of 18 and 35. It can be aggressive—beginning in the testicle, proceeding to the abdomen, chest, and finally the brain.

CT scans and blood work would diagnose the progression of the cancer, but no matter the stage, the first step would be an orchiectomy—the removal of the cancerous testicle.

By 3:00 p.m. I was in surgery. I stayed overnight and was discharged at 1:00 p.m. the next day.

Two weeks later I sat in the exam room of a hospital in New York. This hospital was well known for its treatment of cancer. My surgeon in St. Louis sent me there saying, "It's the best for testicular cancer."

Two doctors, a nurse practitioner, and then my oncologist examined me. Such personal, below-the-belt exams became commonplace. Being unmarried, and a shy type of guy, I knew that no one besides my momma had seen all that was Andrew Mann. Over the next several months I felt as though I had to drop my pants for anyone who walked through the exam room door!

My oncologist was the chief of medicine. He was affable and avuncular. Each visit he would sit in a chair, leaning back, often with hands behind his gray hair. Talking with him felt like talking with a distant, yet familiar member of my family.

The nurse practitioner was a younger woman with blonde hair, a warm smile, and a friendly disposition. She was a nurturer. Always present with my oncologist, she would circle behind and offer to answer any questions after he left the room.

My doctor reviewed with me the labs and scans performed before my surgery. They indicated the cancer had already spread to some lymph nodes in my abdomen. I actually had two types of cancer cells in my body. Therefore, the treatment my doctor recommended was twofold.

First, the embryonal carcinoma cells would require a regime of "EP chemotherapy"—the drugs Etoposide and Cisplatin (EP) would be administered by infusion.

These drugs, however, would have no effect on the teratoma, the other type of cancer cells in my body. Those cells would have to be surgically removed after chemotherapy.

Chemo was tough. A cycle involved five days of treatment followed by a two-week rest period. The first cycle was outpatient. Each morning I traveled to the clinic and had an IV placed in my hand, a process that would become more and more difficult as my veins shrank. I would roam the Internet on my tablet as poison pumped into my body for three or four hours.

Of course what goes in has to come out. I was told to drink a lot of water. This would protect my kidneys as I excreted the poison out of my system. Being the people-pleasing type, I was determined to exceed the hydration quota they gave. As a result I frequently visited the restroom with an IV cart in tow.

After several days of treatment, the smell of the bathroom repulsed me. The slightly floral, chemical odor would make me nauseated. The smell of the alcohol rubbed on my skin before placing an IV would do the same. These smells would continue to trigger my nausea, even a year after treatment.

Persistent nausea was a miserable feeling, but it wasn't the only side effect of treatment. Nausea led to vomiting.

Then there were the hiccups. The word *hiccup* is an understatement. They were more like full-body spasms. They would not only keep me up all night but also bring the stomach juices up into my throat and mouth. I vomited until there was no longer anything left in my stomach.

Many drugs were given to combat the side effects—some were effective, others weren't. To this day a brown paper bag of prescription drugs, abandoned due to their ineffectiveness, sits in my apartment.

By the second cycle of treatment, my nurse practitioner insisted that all future infusions be administered in-patient. One doctor commented, "We're going to keep fluids in you and schlog you out with meds. You may not even remember any of this."

Some things I remember vividly. Like the night Hurricane Sandy hit, when the nurse came in and closed the blinds. I asked, "Why are you closing the blinds?"

She replied, "To protect you from the hurricane."

I couldn't help but think, *What good would a few thin pieces of vinyl do to protect me from 100-mile-per-hour winds?*

I guess the blind might have protected me from shattering glass.

Other things I only saw through the fog of "chemo brain."

On a Friday during one of my off weeks, I went down to lower Manhattan. Hungry, I walked into a restaurant to eat but decided I wanted something different. I walked several blocks to another place but changed my mind again. Standing in line at another restaurant, I decided I wanted to go back to the first. On the street between the two, I turned back to the previous and then back again to the original. I couldn't make up my mind. I felt crazy.

That's "chemo brain."

The third cycle was delayed, allowing time for my diminished white blood cell count, which had dropped, to recuperate. Once treatment began though, this cycle was easier than the first two.

Then came Thanksgiving. I was determined to join family and friends for the festivity. However, most of my time was spent asleep in the bedroom.

During my fourth and final cycle the side effects were stronger than ever. Therefore they gave me more medications, filling my brown paper bag.

Following chemotherapy, blood work and CT scans were performed to determine the treatment's effectiveness.

The results were good. The drugs had done their job. My blood work indicated that the embryonal carcinoma was gone from my body.

The CT scan, however, showed something unexpected. The teratoma in my abdomen had grown. In August the two lymph nodes had been one centimeter and three centimeters, respectively. Now they had merged together and were roughly ten centimeters in length. The tumor had enveloped around and invaded my kidney.

The plan for treatment from the beginning included a follow-up surgery. Now, though, it would be more difficult and included a risk of losing my kidney.

The retroperitoneal lymph node dissection (RPLND) was quite invasive. The surgeon began cutting below my sternum, continued around my belly button, and came to a halt a few inches below. I have a gnarly scar that would make for a good story in a biker bar.

The large incision allowed all of my insides to be removed from my abdomen and set on my chest. I so wish I had a picture of that!

This allowed careful dissection of the tumor that surrounded my kidney as well as the removal of all the lymph nodes from my abdomen, just in case they were cancerous.

After five hours I emerged from my anesthesia-inflicted stupor. A smiling nurse said something as I opened my eyes. I don't remember what.

I asked, "Do I have both my kidneys?"

She said, "Yes you do."

As the anesthesia continued to wear off, I noticed the arterial line plastered to the side of my neck, two IVs running into my hand, and a catheter.

The next week was spent in the hospital recovering. Five o'clock the morning after surgery, I was awakened by a nurse and told to walk a lap around the hospital wing. Instructed to do 15 laps each day, my zealousness to please set in, and I had done my quota by midday. They told me to do 15 more!

Nurses would come and go every hour. In between visits I would press the button of my pain-controlled analgesia (PCA)—a machine that administered doses of pain medication on my command. The pain wasn't too bad considering the 65 staples down my front looked like I had been part of a magic trick gone wrong.

Recovery from surgery also included a precise eating regime. For three days no food or drink were allowed. My bowels had been paralyzed with anesthesia. They were waiting for them to "wake up." Looking for evidence of my bowel's arousal, every doctor asked the same question, "Have you passed gas yet?"

The people pleaser that I am, I was delighted when I could answer, "Yes!" Never before and never since has anyone been so pleased with my flatulence.

Fluids were slowly reintroduced, followed by food. For a month I was on a minimal fat diet in order to prevent ascites, a painful and dangerous infection.

Follow-up visits with my surgeon later became checkups with my oncologist. Oncologist visits became less frequent.

My cancer was gone, gone due to the attention and expertise of top-notch medical care.

However, the Great Physician did so much more than just heal me physically.

CHAPTER

MY STORY—THE STRUGGLE CHAPTER

"Dad is in a mood. I still get so frustrated with him. It is hard to ignore. I don't know what to do to make the situation better."

When I was young, my father managed a bank whose clientele were primarily farmers. His office was in a redbrick building in the center of town. Many moments of my childhood were spent in this place after school and in the summer, with him at his desk and me on the floor playing with my Hot Wheels cars. My boyhood mind fantasized about tales and adventures. I would run in and out of the entrance to the building while the white door with a powerful spring hinge slammed behind me. Depending on the day, I was either Indiana Jones or Donatello, the ninja turtle.

At some point this all changed. I stopped going there. He did too. He began working in a makeshift office set up in the basement of our home. Later this office was moved to a portable storage building in our front yard.

Now, while he worked, I lay on my belly across the giant, yellow, vinyl beanbag that sat in our basement. My eyes were glued to the television, hands busily moving, playing Teenage Mutant Ninja Turtles on the Nintendo.

Sometimes I would turn off the television and look at the family pictures organized in albums that sat nearby on a shelf. Seeing my sister, brother, mom, and dad on family vacations, I wondered, *Why don't I get to go to those places?* My dad seemed happier in those pictures.

What I lacked the ability to understand at the time was that my dad had resigned his job at the bank. His superiors had required him to enforce mandates he believed were unfair to the farmers. Therefore, he quit his job and became self-employed. First a real-estate appraiser, he later became a horse-trailer dealer as well.

My dad's decision meant a big shift for my family, but most of all for him. Being self-employed meant the financial security of his family rested entirely on his shoulders. This weight grew day by day, year after year.

The burdens always seemed to lift when he rode his horse, sometimes by himself, other times with a group of friends, but most frequently with his family.

I began riding horses at age three. Sitting on a pad that rested behind my dad's saddle, my small fingers clinched his belt as we navigated the trails across the Ozarks of Missouri. Although we didn't travel to those far-off places I saw in the pictures, each June we joined about a thousand other trail riders next to the Jacks Fork River for a week of camping, swimming, and of course riding horses.

Looking back, I certainly didn't help ease my father's burdens. Like many teenagers, I was self-centered. I wanted a car at 16. I insisted on attending college in New York City. I wanted a nicer car to travel back and forth to Chicago after transferring to a school there. All of this came at a cost. Of course, there was the financial cost, but the greater toll was my dad's mental well-being.

His sense of worth as a man, as a human being, was directly connected to his ability to provide for his family. So, as I asked for more, he gave more, and the weight grew.

We also butted heads often. My dad was never one to keep his opinion silent. I never had to wonder what he was thinking. He was quick to offer advice, noting many things I could do better. Frequent emails were sent with the subject line: "Idea" or "Suggestion." Here are a few. (Note: Proof is my professional therapy dog. More about her later.)

I know the Piedmont church is getting their shoe boxes ready to go today. Probably other churches are also. You might consider either recording a note to send to the churches or work out a way to make a call to some of the churches while they are having services to let them know your feelings about the work they have done in helping get the boxes to you. The smaller churches do not do much of the high tech stuff, but this might be a touch from you that they would remember. Think about it. Have a good day. —Dad.

Andrew, just saw a commercial on TV for dog food treats and the main character was a dog. Made me think that you should make a contact with the dog food manufacturer that makes the dog food you feed Proof. Maybe they would be interested in using a "real" working dog in promoting their dog food, especially in a big market like NYC, and maybe beyond. You likely know more about how to go about doing something like that than I would. It may not be feasible after given some thought, but it would not hurt to give it a try. You already have video to back up what you would say, and just ask them to Google Proof missionary dog. Have a good day. —Dad.

Andrew, you need to learn the ole gospel song, "I Wouldn't Take Nothing for My Journey Now" on the piano. Sometime when you are preaching or giving some thoughts about what you do you could use this to end the service. I think it would really touch people, and it is a very uplifting song. Think about it. —Dad.

Suggestions would also come after I would speak in churches, telling the story of our ministry center. "You need to slow down when you speak. . . . You need to have Proof do more tricks. . . . You should word it like this . . ."

These comments would make me boil, and I would erupt with harsh, stinging words. Even as an adult, I was still self-centered, careless about his feelings, and always judging his motives.

My relationship with my father was one that I consistently viewed as a struggle. My journal entry from August 18, 2011, reflects this internal conflict: "Dad is in a mood. I still get so frustrated with him. It is hard to ignore. I don't know what to do to make the situation better."

It was written during a trip to Hot Springs, Arkansas. During most of that trip, my dad isolated himself from my mom and me. His mind was overwhelmed. Although his struggle was visible, I looked at it differently. In my perspective he was ruining my vacation.

Because of my self-centered perspective, I had little compassion.

Because I was focused on finding my own immediate, finite pleasure, I did little to intentionally relieve my father's worry. I never once spoke faithful words to help him see again eternal truths that had been the foundation of his life.

Because I wasn't satisfied with my experience, I was unable to help him find eternal satisfaction—upside-down joy.

Because I didn't know all that was on his mind, I was harsh and judging.

I never dared to consider the struggles I experienced in my relationship with my father were shaping me into the man I would become. I now have a different perspective.

4

MY STORY—THE DEATH CHAPTER

"Andrew, something happened. . . . Your dad passed away."

The night before I heard these words, I received this email from my dad: "23 degrees in NYC. 31 degrees in Fairdealing, Missouri. Have a good day. Look forward to seeing you on the morrow. Dad."

The following Monday morning I sat in the passenger seat of an airplane at LaGuardia waiting for takeoff. I was heading home. As is my routine, I dialed my dad's cell phone to let him know my flight was leaving on time. If my parents left their house when I left New York City, we would arrive in St. Louis at about the same time.

He didn't pick up. I wasn't alarmed. I dialed my mom's phone. She didn't pick up. I dialed the home phone. No one picked up. I tried his phone again.

No success.

Now slightly alarmed, but knowing sometimes my parents leave their phones unattended, I dialed my sister's phone, then my brother-in-law's, then their home. No one responded. With my concern raised and the flight attendant telling passengers to turn off their phones, my phone rang.

My brother-in-law was on the other end.

"Andrew, something happened."

I had a bad feeling in the pit of my stomach.

"OK."

"Your dad passed away."

Knowing what he said but not wanting to believe it I asked, "What did you say?"

Fighting back tears, he repeated, "Something happened, and your dad passed away."

I had no words, but managed to say, "OK. I will see you guys soon."

I turned my phone off shortly after the plane took off.

I sat on the plane riding a roller coaster of emotions. With three hours of silence and little interaction with others, I wondered what had happened. I needed a distraction, so I got out my tablet and played Monopoly.

After arriving in St. Louis, I sat in a chair outside baggage claim with my dog. My mom, sister, and brother-in-law arrived about three hours later.

They pulled up to the passenger pickup of the airport. It was gray and rainy outside. I loaded my suitcase in the back of their SUV and sat next to my mom in the backseat. There was little to say except what could be communicated by a tearful hug.

Silence eventually gave way to explanation. They told me what happened after my dad sent me the email.

He went to bed early. My mom stayed up to get the house ready for the homecoming of her baby boy. Not wanting to disturb my dad, she went to sleep in a different room.

The next morning my mom got up and started getting ready. She didn't notice him in the house, but that wasn't unusual. He typically stirred early and busied himself with his routine chores of feeding the horses and doing random jobs around the farm.

My mom became curious when she saw my dad's wallet and keys sitting on the dining room table. She started looking around. Walking into his bedroom, she saw his feet on the floor on the other side of the bed.

She called the paramedics and then my sister.

To this day I can't imagine my mom's experience. Living far outside of town, no one would arrive for at least 30 minutes, leaving my mom sitting next to my lifeless father, the man she had been married to for 44 years.

The paramedics, my sister, and my brother-in-law all arrived at about the same time. This was also about the time I began calling. Knowing I was aboard a plane heading their way, they didn't know whether to answer the phone and tell me the somber news before takeoff or after I landed.

The coroner later concluded what we suspected. My dad died of a seizure during the night. This wasn't his first seizure. One time around Thanksgiving, a seizure scared all of us when his words became senseless and he seemed to black out. We insisted that he go to the doctor. Not one to make a big to-do about his health, he reluctantly complied.

Kind of like a broken car that works fine when being checked out by a mechanic, the doctors never found the cause of his problems. They gave him some medicine to take. Sometimes he took it; sometimes he didn't.

The seizure on his final night caused a massive stroke. His body seized; he rolled out of bed and landed face down in the position my mom found him the next morning.

My family shared this information with me as we made the wet, three-hour drive home from the airport.

Two days later my brother and his family arrived.

The following day was visitation.

The next was the funeral.

My dad always enjoyed entertaining others. I remember him in my childhood walking around the house singing and dancing the old The Big Bopper song, "Chantilly lace, a pretty face, a pony tail, a hangin' down" (written by Jerry Foster, Bill Rice, and J.P. Richardson).

Later as a sixth grader, I participated with a friend in a talent show at our elementary school. We performed the Roy Orbison song, "Pretty Woman." I played piano. My friend sang. My dad came out dressed like a woman!

My dad's flair for entertainment attracted him to the music of a rock 'n' roll-playing, show organist who was also a pastor in Memphis. As the president of a horse breed association, my dad was largely responsible for two horse shows each year. He thought the music of this organist was a perfect match for the breed of horse he loved. So my dad hired him to play music at the shows. The two became friends.

This friend came to the funeral. The same music that put a wiggle in my dad's step at horse shows was played from the same organ at my dad's funeral.

The gospel was shared as well. God was glorified.

Following the funeral, a caravan of cars drove 30 miles to a veterans' cemetery where his ashes were buried. For many, the cracks of gunshots fired by a firing squad at a military funeral reverberate in the heart with echoes of hopelessness. As I listened and the folded red, white, and blue flag was handed to my mom, a lot of things seemed uncertain.

There was a lot I didn't understand. However, through his death, I began to understand the certainty of hope that sprouts from the root of faith.

CHAPTER

THE REAL STORY

I don't think that, as a boy, I was very different from other children. I would dream about the life I would one day have. I wanted to be a rich doctor, respected by all those around me. I drew a picture of my house. It had a basketball court, bowling alley, movie theater, and pipe organ. In the center of that picture was me with a big smile.

At a young age, I started writing that story. I took control of my life, penning a story that focused on my worth, fulfillment, and pleasure. The story was centered on me, being written by me, with my own limited perspective.

Such a finite perspective views sin, sickness, struggle, and death as circumstances to ignore, excuse, avoid, or dread. After all, these things bring pain. It's only natural to maximize pleasure and minimize pain.

In some areas of our lives, we recognize the gain that comes from pain. For example, my sister plays sports, runs, and exercises daily—she has always been in better shape than me. While on vacation one summer, I decided I would work out with her at five o'clock each morning. We did a high-energy, calisthenics-filled, 40-minute DVD workout! Oh the noises that came from our family room as we stood before the television: breathing, grunting, moaning, and complaining.

I used to think, *Why would anyone do such a thing?* Now as I exercised, I thought, *This is torture! I can't do anymore. Push yourself. Just one more. It'll be worth it. Your plump belly is going to be rock-solid.* Later I would look at myself in the mirror thinking, *Are those abs I'm seeing?*

It's tough to have the same perspective with the experiences of our lives that turn our world upside down. An end-focused view is difficult because we don't know how it will all turn out; we don't know how it will end. Therefore we assert control and try to write a story that maximizes our pleasure, a story in which we control the ending. After all, we are the authors of our own stories.

Or, so we think.

Another story is being written by another Author.

The story isn't about us; it's about Him.

It's a story that was, is, and is yet to come. At times the story appears to be a mystery; however, the Author isn't anonymous, writing under a pseudonym, but instead actively revealing Himself within the story. The clues are all around us.

Nevertheless, we have a hard time tracing the lines of the story back to Him. Not wanting us to stay in the dark, the Author inserted Himself into the story. The words of the story became flesh (John 1:14). He revealed Himself as a character in the story. Although the timeline of the story isn't such that I get to meet Him, shake His hand, and audibly hear His voice, I have a greater gift. I can have Him in me. He can become part of my character. One day, we will be indistinguishable. With Him in me, I no longer need to worry about writing my story.

I am incapable of writing the story He is writing. I can't write this story for myself, much less the stories of billions of people who have come before me, are around me, and will come after me.

In the story He is writing, He's not interested in gratifying us with temporary happiness, shallow satisfaction, or empty notions of self-worth. Instead, He's writing a grander story of redemption that concludes with eternal satisfaction—complete joy.

We are all unqualified to write our stories because our perspectives are limited. In our limited perspectives, it makes sense to find the quickest route to pleasure that avoids the most pain. But our Author's perspective is different. He knows we will never experience eternal satisfaction, joy, if we don't change.

So, He is writing a story we would never write.

> *August 18, 2011*
> *"Dad is in a mood. I still get so frustrated with him. It is hard to ignore. I don't know what to do to make the situation better."*
>
> *December 19, 2011*
> *"Andrew, something happened. . . . Your dad passed away."*
>
> *August 27, 2012*
> *"We found a mass. It looks like testicular cancer."*
>
> *July 27, 2014*
> *"For 16 years of my life, I have been disobedient. I need to be right before God and before my church. I need to be baptized."*

I never would have written any of these scenes. Why would I choose to have a strained relationship with my father and then have him unexpectedly die? Why would I make myself sick with the poisons of chemotherapy? Why would I admit I was trapped in a lie? Each one is a vivid memory representing sin, sickness, struggle, and death. Each one turned my world upside-down. Some of those scenes have been great, others small; some short, others long; a few public, many private.

As my tale has unfolded, others stories have been interwoven with mine. These tales of friends, many facing even more daunting challenges than mine, have shaped my own understanding of the story our Author is writing.

None of these scripts would have been written by any one of us. Instead, they were written by an Author that is accomplishing more than we dare ask, hope, or imagine.

I never imagined through admitting sin, God would provide new life. He changed the way I thought. I went from being a master of religion, concerned about what others thought, to being obedient to Jesus. I only cared what He thought!

I never asked God to heal my soul. I didn't know I needed it. However, through cancer, the Great Physician brought more than just physical healing.

I never dared to consider the struggles I experienced in my relationship with my father were shaping me into the man I would become. I now have a different perspective.

Then when my dad died, there was a lot I didn't understand. However through his death, I began to understand the certainty of hope that sprouts from the root of faith.

Many chapters have been written. Many more are yet ahead. I'm not the author, God is.

Each word, sentence, paragraph, chapter, and volume penned with a single purpose in mind: lasting, eternal satisfaction—complete joy.

ABOUT THE AUTHOR

Now a pastor and missionary in the South Bronx, I was initially drawn to the city by the bright lights of Broadway. Growing up in small-town Missouri, I had more experience with horse shows than Broadway shows; nevertheless, I was attracted to the city. As a kid I remember watching *Wheel of Fortune* with my parents and rooting for the contestants to win the "all-expenses-paid trip to New York City."

Although I never experienced much live theater in my early years, the most memorable movie moments for me involved the main characters breaking out in song and dance, like the scene in *Blues Brothers* with Aretha Franklin in the middle of that dingy diner. In my fantasies, in the stories I write in my mind's eye, I imagine epic moments of life celebrated with tap dancing, a chorus line, and me at the center of it all.

I love to sing and dance. The problem is I can't do either, at least well. So instead I play the drums.

Had I been the writer of my story, I would have attended school, auditioned for orchestras, played percussion in Broadway pits, learned to dance, developed a singing voice, and become a headliner on Broadway with my name on the marquee next to Idina Menzel and Kristin Chenoweth's. Perhaps I would have gained the whole world but lost my soul.

Instead, another Author was writing the story. His story is much better. It involved a family friend slipping me a phone number—a contact in the city—a week before heading to college in New York. I needed that phone number when in my first week culture shock had me desperate for comfort. Like fresh air to my gasping lungs, the person on the other side of the phone invited me to his office, took time to pray for me, and directed me to a church.

The next Sunday morning I found myself walking to church past homeless men lying on cardboard. That church was like nothing I had ever experienced. Its ministry and its people captivated me, not with a shiny shell, but with richness of sincerity, genuineness, and meaning.

The next four years were spent studying music at schools in both New York and Chicago. However, my experiences with ministry in those urban environments were just as valuable to me as my education. Experiences in the Humboldt Park neighborhood of Chicago and the Lower East Side of Manhattan shaped who I was and who I wanted to be.

After graduating college, the pastor of the church in New York invited me to begin a new work in the South Bronx. The story has continued, line by line, page by page.

It's easy to look back on the past and see the Author's deft penmanship. Despite this perspective, my tendency is still to grasp for pen to write the next page. Instead, the Author says, "Use that effort to get to know Me."

Religion tends to be the method by which we try to know our Author. All religion, no matter its form, is simply the characters of the story trying to explain the story. With good intentions those that have captured a glimpse of a larger story try to help others see the same. It's a little like trying to explain the ocean to one who has never experienced it. Its vastness and beauty are truly unfathomable until a person stands before it, listening to the crashing waves.

Most of my life has been viewed through the lens of Christian religion. My father was a deacon and my mom was a church nursery worker. I have attended church from birth and eventually became a missionary and pastor. I was a master of religion, but this didn't mean I knew the Author, or at least not well.

Despite memorizing Scripture, reciting stories, and singing songs, I never stood at the shore of my Author's greatness until I was confronted with experiences that turned my world upside down, until I was confronted with sin, sickness, struggle, and death.

Through those upside-down circumstances I began to see, not as one being told what to see, but as one seeing it for myself.

Here are some of the things I know about Him. He is different from me. He has authority. He is graciously loving, and His Word is true—I can trust it.

The difficult circumstances of life have revealed these things, but also another unlikely source has taught me much about Him as well. So much of what I know and understand about my Author, I have learned from my relationship with my dog. Her name is Proof. She's a mild-mannered, yellow Labrador retriever with a soft, puppylike face and a tail that doesn't quit.

At home she is my pet, but when she walks out the door she is my co-worker. She is a certified assistance animal and a professional therapy dog. Trained in a prison facility in Colorado, her life has since been spent living and working with me. Proof's work with kids in the South Bronx has earned her the title "missionary dog." She's certainly not just your average, ordinary pooch.

Her work has gone beyond just helping me help others. She has helped me better understand my Author. She has helped me think about the difference between me and my Author; after all, Proof is different than me.

It's easy to treat dogs like they're human, especially dogs trained as well as Proof. Some people dress their dogs in human clothes, feed them human food, and interpret their dog's behavior through their human rather than canine perspective. Ten out of ten dog experts agree: dogs are different from humans!

Proof and I are innately different. First, I am human, and she is not. Second, my existence preceded hers. My life began long before hers. Alone, each of these characteristics lends me an understanding of the world she will never have, but even more so combined.

The Author of our story is also innately different from us. He is divine, and we are not. This makes Him holy, set apart, different.

He's also eternal. His existence preceded ours.

These two characteristics certainly lend Him an understanding of the world that we will never have.

I have also learned the Author of our story has authority. His authority means He has the ability to author the story. He alone can do this.

We like to think we have authority. We make little kingdoms for ourselves. As children we live in the kingdom of our parents. Then we gain independence, move out, and begin setting up our own kingdoms.

A person walking in my apartment would recognize pretty quickly that it is the kingdom of Andrew Mann. It's not a big kingdom—after all, I'm a missionary living in New York City—but it is mine. In it, my rules reign. But even there I don't have total power. Things happen over which I don't have control.

At three o'clock one morning, I woke up to the smell of smoke and people screaming. Jolting out of bed, I rushed to the window. People were on the street, pointing up at the smoke wafting not far from my window.

A typical icebreaker question is, *In the event of a fire, what three things would you take with you?* I don't have to wonder. I know. I grabbed my phone, my computer, and my dog and headed for the door.

It turned out the building next to me was on fire. My apartment was fine.

It's clear, though, that I don't have total control.

The Author of our story does. He always has, and always will. He will never lose control. We can be certain of that because He is all-powerful and all-knowing.

Our Author's supreme power and wisdom give Him rightful authority. He is in control of the story.

The story He is writing isn't about the kingdom of Andrew Mann but rather His kingdom. Living in this kingdom is the only path to eternal satisfaction, to true joy.

Too often we search for satisfaction by building our own kingdoms. We try to make the most of our life. We think this means getting as much as we can. We work hard to get a lot of things: friends, food, money, clothing, girlfriends, boyfriends, spouses, education, career, houses, cars, success, respect, love, and legacy. To obtain these ends, we assert control. We assume the authority.

Some live another way. They live in another person's kingdom, giving someone else power and authority. I see this on the streets of the Bronx when a teenage girl asserts control of her life and tries to obtain from boys the attention she has been missing.

Living in my own kingdom or in someone else's will never end with joy. It will never lead to satisfaction. It ends with the opposite of joy: heartache.

Heartache is the pain that comes from knowing there's something better. After all, there has got to be more than the kingdoms that I or anyone else can build.

Living life in the city, I have found something better. My life in the city has helped me realize the city is a beautiful place. That's not often what people see on first glance.

Many only see heartache in the city. They don't have to look hard to see it. It's evident when they walk the street dodging the scattered dog poop, hearing sirens, and smelling the skunklike odor of pot wafting from a window.

I, too, see heartache in the city. I see it when neighbors cursing, screaming, and fighting interrupt quiet evenings watching television. I saw it one time when I looked out the peep hole of my door and saw two men rolling down the stairs, one tackled by the other during a melee. Heartache has awakened me in the night with the crack of a gunshot.

That's what I primarily saw at first. However, sometimes it takes time for us to see things as they really are. Sometimes we have to look under the dust to see the beauty of an old car. Sometimes we have to look deeper.

In my neighbors I have witnessed great resiliency, compassion, and care. I have come to better understand what it means to, "Love your neighbor as yourself" (Matthew 22:39). They have shown that love to me.

Frequently I soak in all my experiences and think, *This has got to be a little taste of heaven.* Many people think city life is complex and harsh. But mine is actually simple. I don't own a house; instead, I rent an apartment. It's nothing fancy. It's a one-bedroom apartment on the fourth floor of a five-story building. Out of my back window, I can see cars going back and forth on the busy Bruckner Expressway. Others' kingdoms are probably larger. After all, I don't even own a car. I walk or ride my bike.

But I wonder if others have found what I have found. I wonder if they have freedom, true freedom. I wonder if they know their neighbors. I wonder if their lives are meaningful. I wonder if they are satisfied. I wonder if they are joyful.

My simple way of living has shaped my understanding of my Author's kingdom. It has helped me live with the end in mind, to live upside down.

I may not own much, but I do feel great freedom. I do know my neighbors; I pass them on my way to work, to church, and to the grocery store. My life is meaningful. I am satisfied. I have joy.

I have found my heaven on earth in an unexpected corner of New York City, a corner where many only see sin, sickness, struggle, and death.

Yes, my heart aches for those around me who have yet to see beyond their own sin, sickness, struggle, and death. It hurts for those I see on the expressway of life busily building their own kingdoms. But I trust the Author who knows more than me, who is more powerful than me, and who has all authority. He is doing in their life what He has done in my life. He is using the upside-down circumstances—even sin, sickness, struggle, and death—to grow His kingdom and to write His story.

7 THE STORY WITHIN THE STORY

The majority of my days are spent living in and loving the city. A couple of times each year, I return home to the small Missouri farm where most of my family lives. Here the greatest busyness comes not from tourists in Times Square but from dozens of hummingbirds that swarm the syrup-filled, red feeders. Miles outside of a tiny town, with only one neighbor in sight, this 45-acre plot is a place of rest, recovery, and refreshment for my soul.

The house sits at the top of a small hill from which most of the property can be seen. One of my favorite places to sit is on the front porch, gently rocking back and forth on the swing that hangs from above. From this perch I can see horses grazing in the tall amber grass with hues of green and purple below towering pine trees from which the property gets its name, M Pines. At the bottom of one of the horse pastures is a small body of water dubbed by my dad as "Andrew's Pond." Being a farm pond, it can be slightly muddy with slimy green algae at times. Within that pond exists an entire world, an ecosystem not natural to the property but created by the original owners of the property.

The fish of that pond—stocked bluegill, bass, and catfish—live their lives totally unaware of the world that exists around them. Only when someone decides to go fishing do the fish jarringly become aware of the existence of life outside their little world.

Our human experience isn't much different. Living in this fish tank of a world, our perspective tends to be as finite as a fish's. Like fish in a muddy pond, we lack the ability to understand the world outside of ours. We are limited by the world where we find ourselves. We want more but don't know how to find it. Sometimes our limited perspective prevents us from realizing a frog we encounter in our pond doesn't come from our world, it comes from another. Sometimes, though, we experience moments that transcend our existence. We become curious when a frog swims across the water, thinking, *Surely there's more than just this pond of a world!*

Sometimes we see these eternal frogs when our knowledge can't explain the feelings we have from nature, relationships, experiences, fellowship, or community. These feelings alone are certainly self-evident of eternity. They are an Author revealing Himself within the story, and we have already discussed how this Author is different from us and how he has rightful authority.

Love is another characteristic intrinsic to His nature. He abounds in love for us, the characters of His story. His love is such that He doesn't leave us wondering about the frogs which come across our life. Because of His love, He has gone to great lengths so we might know Him.

His Word, His Story became flesh and lived with us. He inserted himself into the story, He jumped into the pond. We now know Him as Jesus. Jesus walked the shores beyond our pond, in the land of eternity. His life in this world was lived in constant awareness of the reality that existed beyond. He taught all those around Him eternal truths.

He was like us but also different from us. He called himself the Son of Man; yet, at the same time, He talked about His Father in heaven. He saw all of His life, the good and the bad, under the authority of His Father. Therefore, for Him, nothing took precedence above His relationship to His Father.

This relationship was not exclusive for Him. The events that took place during His earthly life would allow all of humanity the ability to become children of His Father.

Like our fish friends in the pond, we will never understand without the Author revealing Himself to us. This revelation has happened, is happening, and will happen.

It *happened* through the life of Jesus.

It *is happening* now as God reveals Himself to me and the other fish of this world through His Word.

It *will happen* one day when the waters of this world dry up, and everyone sees that Jesus is indeed Lord.

A lot of what I know about the Author—He is different from me, He has authority, He is graciously loving—I have learned through the circumstances of life that turned my world upside down. But I didn't have to experience these sin, sickness, struggle, and death to know these truths. They can be found in His Word. It is true—I can trust it.

The Author's story has been written for us to read. First given to the nation of Israel, it seemed at first only to relate to them. But that wasn't the whole story. All they learned about Him found its fulfillment in Jesus. If words are how we make known what is in our mind, then Jesus was indeed the Word. He made known what was in His Father's mind.

Of course, the Author's mind had been previously revealed through prophets. After Jesus, apostles would do the same. But Jesus was unique. He didn't merely communicate the words of God, but became the bridge by which we step from the pond to the unlimited shore of eternity.

The prophets, apostles, and Jesus' words are found in the Bible. Many skeptics question its veracity, but I have found it can be trusted. So many of the truths I have learned through sin, sickness, struggle, and death, I now read in the Bible. They were there the whole time.

There is a central theme throughout the entire Bible. This theme provides perspective when facing sin, sickness, struggle, and death.

Here it is: live with the end in mind. In other words, live upside down.

I was reminded of this while sitting in a tight seat at the Neil Simon Theater on Fifty-Second Street and Broadway. With a cackle in her voice, the witch in the Broadway musical *Big Fish* sang, "Everyone dies, Edward Bloom. But your death is glorious. Let me show you."

In her crystal ball she showed Edward how his life would end. I don't know what he saw, but this revelation changed Edward. It became a catalyst for a life of adventure. His flamboyant tales of a giant, a mermaid, a werewolf, and heroism seem at best fictitious hyperbole, at worst vain lies. After all, how could anyone experience such fullness of life?

Perhaps the words of the witch answer this question: "Life begins when you know how it ends."

Knowing the end informs how to live life now.

The concept is simple. The end informs the beginning and the middle. Carpenters know what a table will be before it is built; contractors operate off a blueprint designed by an architect; bakers know the taste and design of the cake before they start.

How then would we know the substance of a good life if we don't know how good it should taste in the end?

Our Creator tells us to "Taste and see that [He] is good" (Psalm 34:8). He wants our life now to be fat from eternity. The only way to get fat is from eating. So often our life is spent consuming the pleasures of this world yet that leaves our soul—the thing that lasts forever—emaciated and malnourished. Instead, our Author has given us a Word that is saturated with the eternal. By consuming it, we fatten our soul. Like a sponge whose purpose isn't found until it is saturated with water, our lives miss their true meaning before they are saturated with the eternal.

Eternity is hard to imagine. I can stick my wet finger in sand. If I look closely, I can focus on just one grain. I can try to count all the surrounding grains, but I never make it very far before I stop. Eternity isn't comparable to all the grains of sand on my finger. It isn't even comparable to all the grains of sand on all the beaches in the entire world. Its days are uncountable, numberless.

So, rather than focus on the life found in this grain of sand, focus on the end.

How does it end?

The Author has told us in His Word. He will be worshipped. His worshippers will be entirely devoted to Him. They will live in total freedom, yet total subordination. They will serve as slaves, yet reign as kings and queens forever.

This is only the outcome for people who connect to that eternal reality while living this temporary existence. It's only the end for those who choose to live in His kingdom now. Those that don't will finally see the truth and will even worship the Creator, but will be sentenced to a second, eternal death.

The only way to know if this description of the end is true is if the One who is eternal, with all knowledge and power, tells us.

Jesus did just that. He told us how the story ends. In the end He is worshipped forever, as He is the only One deserving. His Word tells us to do now what we will do forever—worship Him. We are to live with eternity in mind, in other words upside down. By living this way we can experience now what we will experience forever—joy.

BETWEEN THE BEGINNING AND THE END

Monotony, boredom, desperation, and depression are all linked to limited pleasure in a limited world. Busyness, hustle, angst, and anxiety are the result of our attempts to acquire all the pleasure we can. For people who focus on building their kingdom, these words describe their everyday life. However, in God's kingdom we experience life every day.

No one wants to feel bad; we all want to feel good. A taste of good leads us to be hungry for more. We are hard-wired as addicts, addicted to pleasure.

In my South Bronx neighborhood, this intrinsic characteristic of humanity is seen as people smoke cigarettes, line up at the liquor store, or roll a joint. I don't have to look far, though, to find it in my own life.

Not long ago I began drinking coffee. For most of my life, coffee had no appeal to me, but I knew many others found great pleasure in it. Seeking my own pleasure, I first began with sweet, froufrou, blended drinks. It didn't take long for me to end up on the other end of the spectrum, finding pleasure in the third-wave coffee movement, drinking it straight black. A mug of hot java is now a routine part of my morning.

Our addiction to pleasure leads us to spend our life acquiring the things that give us pleasure. Money itself doesn't give pleasure, but the sense of worth it gives and the things it buys provide for many of the fixes we need. But most people find that this alone doesn't meet their cravings; something more powerful is needed.

Seeking a new high, we may turn to relationships as the drug of choice. Relationships have the ability not only to scratch our itch for physical connection but also to fill a reservoir of desire to know and be known, to care and be given care, to love and be loved.

Like peeling back the layers of an onion, finding pleasure at each of these levels only makes a person aware that there are deeper levels of pleasure. They realize they are not satisfied.

Many search for something more. Religious people, no matter their background, are like addicts looking for a drug that will give a deeper, more meaningful high. Some people seem to find something to appease their cravings, but even these aren't totally fulfilled.

The desire for pleasure and satisfaction isn't embedded deep within our nature by random chance or evolutionary progression. It was written into our nature by the Author and Creator Himself. It's one of the frogs swimming across the pond of our life. If we follow the frog, our desires will take us to the banks of eternity!

Our Creator placed this drive deep within our souls to open our eyes to the real, eternal world outside this temporary one. Our desire isn't for money, relationships, power, prestige, fame, success, worth, or any other limited, short-term pleasure. We long for eternal pleasure. We are all addicts longing for joy.

As a child, I remember a poster in my sixth-grade teacher's classroom. It was an optical illusion. Upon first glance, it seemed to be just a jumbled graphic. I tried to figure it out, but I never saw anything besides what was right in front of my face. One day someone told me not to focus on the image. Instead of looking at it, I should look through it. It worked. A new image appeared.

Joy, purpose, and even meaning in the difficulties of life are found with the same perspective. Not focusing on the struggles, but rather looking through them, seeing the world upside down.

Seeing the world this way, we tap into an eternal reality.

I'm reminded of an artesian well from my childhood. This well was a pipe sticking out of the ground. Our family encountered it while riding our horses in the backwoods of Missouri. To this day I have never tasted water so sweet. At least that's how I remember it.

Water always seemed to run from that well—on hot days and cold days, in rainy weather, and in drought. I reckon that water is still flowing today. The water didn't flow based on the circumstances surrounding the pipe; it flowed because its source was abundant, deep below the surface of the ground.

The Author of the story wants me to drink from His well, a pipeline from eternity. Eternal life isn't only yet to come—it is now. I can experience it by living the same way Jesus lived, in relationship with my Father.

That's what brings my dog, Proof, the most joy. She is most content and satisfied when she is with me. If I leave the room, she begins to panic. She gets anxious. Boy, is she excited to see me when I come into her presence after an absence. Her actions have earned her the nickname Wiggle-Butt, a nicknamed earned because of the excited gyration of her posterior as she expresses her elation to see me return.

Although she has little ability to fully understand, I am the initiator of her purpose. I give meaning to her life. She works for me, accomplishing the purposes I have for her. These purposes are both for her good and for the good of those around her. Those purposes often involve interacting with children who are having a tough day. Honestly, it's not her favorite thing to do, but she willingly obeys . . . most of the time. The catalyst for her obedience is her relationship with me, a relationship she only could have entered into by my search for her many years ago.

That's the story the Author is writing. He is our Creator, the Initiator of our purpose, not only giving life but also giving it meaning. He has good purposes to be accomplished in, and through, our lives. Although we may miss His favor in the midst of trying circumstances, we learn to obey despite difficulty because of our relationship with Him.

As we obey, we learn the Author is using those circumstances for our good in at least two ways.

First, they lead us to search for eternity.

CS Lewis is an author that is particularly adept at explaining eternal realities to noneternal beings. He described our longing for the eternal in his book *Mere Christianity*: "If I find in myself a desire which no experience in this world can satisfy, the most probable explanation is that I was made for another world."

Second, the Author uses the upside-down circumstances of life— even sin, sickness, struggle, and death—to make us something better. For me, and the many stories in this book, we are *something better* not despite but because of confrontations with sin, sickness, struggle, and death.

That's not how we normally view the circumstances that turn our world upside down. So often our prayer is for God to change those circumstances. Perhaps though, He would rather change the lenses through which we see those circumstances. Perhaps He wants to change us!

Jesus helps us to see these circumstances upside down. He had a different way of seeing things. He saw religious leaders as hypocrites, a band of misfits as protégés, and the Cross as a means of displaying His true glory. He saw all things through eternal lenses.

If we wear these lenses, we won't expect to find joy by changing our circumstances, but instead by viewing those same circumstances from an eternal perspective.

Sin isn't merely wrongdoing; it's trading eternal satisfaction for temporary pleasure. We know sickness may eat away at this life, but it wakens us to our eternal souls. Struggle looks different. It may make us feel weak, yet it simultaneously strengthens our spirit. We no longer view death as the end of life; it's the beginning.

Recently my mom underwent treatment to restore her vision. Diabetes had taken a toll on her eyes. She described her sight prior to surgery as being cloudy. She sometimes laughed about her sight. Her favorite commercial was a woman in bed petting a raccoon, thinking it was her cat.

Cloudy vision prevents us from seeing the truth. Sometimes it's hard to distinguish the counterfeit from the truth, the temporary from the eternal. What makes matters worse is we have an adversary plotting against us. His entire scheme is built on our trading eternal satisfaction for temporary pleasure.

Jesus warned us about the adversary. He talked about a thief that steals, kills, and destroys (John 10:10). Jesus knew the thief's tactics because he used them on Him. While fasting in a desert, Jesus was focusing on the eternal reality and His relationship with His Father in that reality. His adversary wanted short-term pleasure to be predominant in Jesus' mind (Matthew 4). He reminded Jesus of His hunger and enticed Him with wealth, fame, and power. Jesus' fight wasn't against His adversary. His fight was to focus on eternity.

A mindset bound by the limitations of a temporary existence naturally leads a person to make the most of life in this world. Unaware of the end, some try to extract every drop of life from their everyday existence.

Eternal satisfaction is not just meant for the life to come. It's something we can connect to now. Ironically I found this truth through the sin, sickness, struggle, and death in my life. I no longer view these things as irony, but as intentionality. My mom underwent surgery to restore her vision, and now she sees more clearly. Difficult circumstances can bring the same clarity, a kind of surgery on the eyes of the soul.

SIN

July 27, 2014: *"For 16 years of my life, I have been disobedient. I need to be right before God and before my church. I need to be baptized."*

On **August 3, 2014,** as a missionary and pastor, I admitted my sin before my church, repented of that sin, and was baptized.

I went from being a master of religion, concerned about what others thought, to being obedient to Jesus. I only cared what He thought!

WHAT WILL PEOPLE THINK?

In the Bible there's a group of people who had a hard time changing the way they thought. Jesus had some blunt words for them. He said, "Woe to you, scribes and Pharisees, hypocrites!" (Matthew 23:13). Why?

> Because they "make long prayers for show . . . travel over land and sea to make one proselyte, and when he becomes one, you make him twice as fit for hell as you are . . . you pay a tenth of mint, dill, and cumin, yet you have neglected the more important matters of the law—justice, mercy, and faith . . . you clean the outside of the cup and dish, but inside they are full of greed and self-indulgence . . . you are like whitewashed tombs, which appear beautiful on the outside, but inside are full of dead men's bones and every impurity . . . on the outside you seem righteous to people, but inside you are full of hypocrisy and lawlessness." (v. 14FF)

He calls them "blind fools," "snakes," and a "brood of vipers."

Their whole life they had studied about God, yet when He appeared before them, in the flesh, they were unable to change the way they thought.

Their thinking was dominated by the same thought that loomed large in my mind for 16 years. The thought that kept me from admitting my sin and getting baptized.

What will people think?

This thought reveals a heart that wants to be worshipped. God says the worship of anything besides Him is idolatry. Therefore, as long as that question reigned in their hearts and minds and as long as it reigned in my heart and mind, we would never be able to please God. Our lives would be marked by sin.

Idolatry is placing anything on the pedestal of our life besides God. It may appear at times that materialism or relationships sit on our throne, but the truth is that the root of all sin is our ascending this pedestal. Craving eternal joy, we find things that make us feel good, things that give us worth, things that brush another layer of gold on the veneer of our life.

In places around New York City, a person can buy a god—a little, gold-painted figurine to worship. That seems so absurd. Yet so much of my life was spent painting myself gold and worshipping my own image.

I enjoyed being on a pedestal. Excelling and being the best gave me pleasure. I was an addict for recognition, honor, and notoriety. That's why I worked hard in school, clamored for the lead roles in the children's musicals, played instruments on the stage of our church, sought leadership positions in clubs at school, and got baptized at an early age. Although I was blind to it then, I wanted to be worshipped.

Perhaps that's why we tend to call dogs "man's best friend." They worship us. My dog, Proof, treats me like a god. Her fondness is evident by the way she wiggles her tail whenever she sees me. I wonder though if she really worships me or worships what I give her. Often it seems her life doesn't center on me; it centers on food. Food is what truly gives her pleasure. She knows in the morning and at night I provide her food. But sometimes her desire for pleasure drives her to search outside our relationship for snacks. She will sniff around on the floor, eating any crumbs she finds.

When the food stops coming in our bowls, we have two options. We can search all around eating anything we can find, or we can draw closer to the One who provides all things.

Proof normally does the first. She doesn't always draw near to me. She doesn't always seek to do my pleasure. It's often her own pleasure she seeks. She worships herself.

How often we find ourselves in the same boat. How often do we wiggle our tail at God but take greater pleasure in the food than we do in Him? How often do we find ourselves not worshipping our Creator and seeking His pleasure, but instead seeking after the pleasures that come from Him as we worship ourselves?

Several signs point to our self-worship, the ascension to the pedestal in our life. These signs indict us, showing our heart is the same as the Pharisees for whom Jesus had such harsh words.

In no particular order, the first of these signs is relativism. Relativism is the denial of absolute truth. We can see relativism in the thought "What's good for you may not be good for me." This thought takes many forms. In the South Bronx, the cliché *YOLO* ("you only live once") has become the flippant mantra of many people. Similar thoughts include *live life to the fullest, take life as it comes, carpe diem* ("seize the day"), and, *Laissez les bons temps rouler!* ("Let the good times roll!"). These philosophies remind me of trying to catch butterflies when I was a kid. With a net I would chase and chase. Finally catching one, it wasn't long before it was dead in the jar.

At their core, each of these relativist thoughts denies an absolute truth, an eternal standard. They deny a God who sits on the throne with all authority, wisdom, and power. These lives assume authority and with limited wisdom and power try to extract the most possible pleasure from life. The denial of deeper truth, of an eternal reality, leads us to do all that we can to make the most of our experience because that's all we are guaranteed. It's the only thing of which we are certain.

Often those that don't stand on any truth will be easily blown to superstition and false truths. I see this in the Bronx when someone crosses themselves as they walk by a church or when I hear someone say, "Don't split the pole, that's bad luck!" I had never heard this phrase until I moved to the city, but apparently if two people, who are walking down the street together, walk on opposite sides of a pole, bad luck is imminent.

Such superstition and false truth isn't much different from religion. Superstition and religion both place undue significance on things that are insignificant, things that have little impact on eternity.

Religiosity is another sign that points to the ascension to the pedestal of our life. Religiosity focuses on outward appearances while ignoring the truth of what's inside. It is a salve that covers the external sore while the inside festers. It is a sign we are sitting on the throne of our life because in God's kingdom the inside is far more important than the outside. Truth matters, not appearances.

The next sign we have ascended to the pedestal of our life is ridicule. Ridicule is elevating one's self above another. It's a sign we are sitting on our throne because we are trying to knock others off of theirs. Ridicule may take the form of gossip, bitterness, a grudge, or discourse within our own mind.

Sometimes we ridicule others publicly, but more frequently we ridicule others in private. When we see them, we smile. Yet we crucify people over and over again in our way of thinking about them. The words of Oswald Chambers have been a healthy reminder for me. In *My Utmost for His Highest,* he said, "Stop having a measuring rod for other people. There is always one fact more in every man's case about which we know nothing."

At the heart of ridicule is the destruction of others. With that in our heart, it's natural to be fearful that others might destroy us. The name for that fear is anxiety.

Anxiety is the fourth sign that we are thinking like a Pharisee by idolizing ourselves. Anxiety is fear of destruction. Anxiety is thinking that some part of us will be destroyed—our body, reputation, worth, security, or even life itself. It's the fear that our kingdom will be destroyed, that our idol of self will be smashed. Anxiety makes its bed in a mind that is focused on finding the most pleasure possible in this life without thought of eternity.

Looking back, I see all these signs in my story. I had made an idol of myself. I was quick to ridicule others. I was anxious to succeed. The standard I expected from others publicly was not a standard I held for myself privately. My lack of integrity was a sign of both relativism and religiosity in my life. I was a master of religion, after all!

Relativism, religiosity, ridicule, and anxiety are all signs that we have ascended to the pedestal of our life, a place we don't belong. The eternal truth is that our Creator and Author alone is worthy of worship. He is on the pedestal. I am not.

10 FINDING ASLAN
IN THE CITY

Through the course of my pharisaical, idolatrous life, God was rich in grace and mercy, helping me change the way I think. He worked through people, circumstances, struggles, and ultimately sin to open my eyes to the truth. He used these things to write the story of my salvation.

Living and working in urban environments for over a decade, I have encountered many people whose lives have raised questions in my mind. Their lives have helped me to think!

Ariel is one of these people.

During my years of attending school outside of Chicago, each Saturday a few friends and I would drive the Eisenhower Expressway east to Kedzie Boulevard. Heading north to Humboldt Park, I would park my red, decade-old Acura at the corner of Potomac and Washtenaw.

There in the upper apartment of a redbrick duplex, several boys ranging in age from 10 to 15 would gather for what we simply called "Bible study."

Each of these boys who came from the immediate surrounding blocks knew the tenant of that duplex. She was a plainspoken, sharp-tongued, ever-caring Mother Teresa of that Chicagoan Calcutta. Her story of connecting to the Author's story took her from street life to eternal life.

Her name was Miss Betty. She invited and welcomed four green, naive, college boys from the suburbs into her apartment to minister to some young guys in a way she thought she couldn't.

Ariel, a short, feisty boy with a bushy Afro, lived with his mom and stepfather, a leader of a gang.

One day years later I spent some time talking with Ariel. Reflecting on his childhood, Ariel said, "I saw how when stuff wasn't right and people did something wrong, my stepfather would beat on them. As a kid I would have to sit there and watch that. I didn't really have a choice."

The other dominant male in Ariel's life was his brother, a father figure whom Ariel followed and admired. But when it became clear to Ariel's mom that his brother was wrapped up in the gang life and would eventually suffer the inevitable fate of prison or death, she moved him to Florida, leaving Ariel feeling alone in the war zone.

Mikey, a jolly, heavy-set, teddy bear type of guy, invited Ariel to Bible Study. Ariel recalls, "I didn't really know what it was, so I asked Mikey. He said it was worshipping God, talking about God, and doing fun things with some young men from the suburbs."

Ariel attended Bible study nearly every Saturday for four years. These couple hours of his week were a stark contrast from the other hours. Ariel had fun playing football, learning about the Bible, and making plays from the stories he read. These activities gave him a glimpse of the eternal. He described it saying, "We were having a beautiful time that I had never had."

In his 'hood, though, it was often hard to see the eternal reality in the midst of commonplace tragedy. Ariel and the other kids, playing in the alley, would run and hide when they heard the sound of shooting. Two of his friends were murdered. One was shot right in front of him. Ariel somberly recalled, "He lay in my lap losing his life." His stepdad was shot as well. Ariel himself was purposely hit by a car because someone thought he was in a rival gang.

Ariel says his greatest victory was not getting wrapped up in the gang life, which the loom of the neighborhood wove all around him.

Just as I have found in my own life, Ariel's greatest battle wasn't external; it was internal, within his mind.

Ariel described this battle when he told me, "I was always thinking, *Why does my cousin, my sister, and my brother have their father and I don't?* When my brother left for Florida, I was really depressed."

Not long after his brother left, Ariel tried to commit suicide. His mom caught him before it happened. "She sent me to the crazy home. She said I needed time alone to think about stuff."

So one night I found myself driving on the familiar Eisenhower Expressway, under the orange city lights to the "crazy home," the hospital where Ariel was being treated.

His mom and his doctor had made arrangements for my visit. Nevertheless, the nurse on the floor that evening refused to allow any visitation. Not sure if she would follow through with my request, I asked her to give a few things to Ariel. I handed the nurse a deck of cards, a picture from a Bulls' game Ariel had attended with other boys from our Bible study, and a Bible.

Back on the expressway, I was disappointed by the outcome of my journey. The ringing of my phone interrupted my thoughts. The screen showed an unfamiliar number. I pulled over to the side of the road and said, "Hello?"

Silence.

"Hello?"

Muted sounds gave way to what was clearly a person crying.

Between sniffles I heard a voice say, "Andrew, I've never known love like this before."

Something in all of us desires love. Throughout our temporary existence on this earth, we sometimes experience echoes from eternity. These experiences are loose threads from the tapestry of eternity. They are designed for us to grasp and trace back to the true eternal reality. Our tendency though is to rip these threads from the eternal fabric. Experiencing them apart from their eternal design leaves us unaware of their source. Not knowing the source, we don't worship the One who deserves it.

That dark night, Ariel grasped one of those threads from eternity. He continued to follow it to its source. He began to understand the story that his Author was writing. A few months later, Ariel connected his story to Jesus' story and committed to follow Him.

After college, I moved to New York City, and years later, I returned to Chicago. During this trip God used Ariel to raise a question in my mind.

What is the gospel?

I spent a day with Ariel and some of the other boys from our Bible Study. We drove through the city, played basketball, and talked about friends. Some of those friends were now in jail.

Without a doubt, I knew Ariel's commitment to follow Jesus had connected him to the true eternal reality. Yet as we spoke that day, Ariel told me things I didn't like to hear. His honesty to me regarding his life of liquor, weed, and sex pointed to a life of idolatry. This life certainly was a contrast from what's expected from those who follow Jesus.

Ariel's sin was apparent, at least to me. Yet it didn't repulse me. I was more troubled by the same sin I saw in the pristine, serene, calm of suburbia, than by what I saw in the concrete jungle. This more troubling sin I saw in myself.

I began asking myself, *What's more displeasing to a holy Creator—the lustful, pleasure-seeking sin of an urban male who has been surrounded by nothing else, or the same sins clothed in religious garb?*

These first two questions led to another.

What does it mean for Ariel to follow Jesus?

So much of my ministry then and still to this day involves empowerment through education and good living. Yet I wondered if this type of ministry only led people to trade one set of shackles for another. Was I helping people build a different type of idol? Was my ministry doing what Jesus warned against? Making people twice as fit for hell as me (Matthew 23:15)!

Many individuals become slaves to success, goal setting, consumerism, and materialism. They become prideful with a false sense of their own abilities. Stories abound of "successful" people committing suicide, having out-of-control children, maintaining or dissolving unhappy marriages, and participating in institutional and generational sins of our culture.

The fault of these kinds of lives is the same as those whose lives look more sinful. They make an idol of themselves. They find temporary, short-lived pleasure apart from the eternal joy of our Author's true reality.

There's a story that has lurked its way across to those who are searching for the true eternal reality. It's a false story. It promotes pristine, polished lives that value image over authenticity. It tells a tale that perfect harmony is more pleasing to God than the failed attempts of an urban teen. This story insists that the Bible is plain when it comes to moral living, yet calls the same word to sell everything one has and give it to the poor as contextual and metaphoric.

I didn't just see others believing this false story; I believed it as well. Believing this story, I was puzzled when the chronology of the story I would write for others was different than the Author's timeline.

At this time in my life, I was blessed to read the tales about the character Aslan in CS Lewis's *The Chronicles of Narnia*. Representing the character of God, Aslan is a good lion, yet not tame. Reading these tales helped change my thinking. Up to that point, I had clearly tried to tame the Lion. I thought I knew how God would work in another person's life. I thought I could write that story.

Yet the Author was still writing that story in my life. What I didn't know at the time, but later learned, was that the people I thought I was saving were actually saving me.

Experiencing life with them helped me see myself differently.

RATS, RACISTS, RACECARS, AND REDEMPTION

Do you see yourself as gold or as dust?

This question was posed to me by a professor in college. My answer was dishonest. Not much different than the pious Pharisees in Matthew 23, I knew how I wanted others to see me, so I responded humbly, "I see myself as dust."

Inside though, I saw myself as gold.

The question is important. Are we dust or are we gold?

Imagine a rat—a big, brown, Norwegian, sewer rat. This isn't hard for me. Such rats are common around the city. Once I had a rat fall off of a building and land less than a foot behind me. To this day I don't know if it was a kamikaze rat aiming for me, or if he simply had a death wish. I can imagine the newspaper headlines: "South Bronx Pastor Killed by Flying Rat."

Add to your image of a rat some clothes, a top hat, and a cane. Give him a pair of spectacles and a pocket watch. Have him walk on two feet rather than four and speak with a British accent. Go ahead and give him a name. My rat's name is Hubert.

Even with Hubert dressed in all this garb and with humanlike mannerisms, I wouldn't invite him to dinner.

Why?

Because I know he is still a rat. Rats do what rats do. They eat trash, run around sewers, and defecate everywhere they go.

God calls us rats, or something like rats. He calls us wicked sinners: "A righteous man eats until he is satisfied, but the stomach of the wicked is empty" (Proverbs 13:25). This is part of our nature. It was the reason even at such an early age I chose to make an idol of myself. It wasn't some elaborate scheme of mine. It was the nature within me. I was a sinner doing what sinners do.

That's only part of the story. We may be sinners, but we are sinners made in the image of our Creator. This makes us unique from the rest of creation.

Because of this nature, we have many of the characteristics of our Creator. Dominion, power, authority, and wisdom are ours. When exercised in relationship with our Creator, in light of eternal truth, these traits please Him. When abused, wielded by people who have made gods of themselves, these traits can have horrific consequences.

On a recent trip to Birmingham, Alabama, I saw sin and its consequences on display in the Civil Rights Museum. The experience was quite moving. Several images still linger in my mind. One picture showed two black men lynched, hanging from a tree, surrounded by white onlookers. Slightly to the left of center stood a young man, smiling at the camera.

Another image that remains in my mind is of a 13-year-old boy. He was killed on the day of the Sixteenth Street Baptist Church bombing. That act of terrorism killed four little girls. But this young man wasn't killed by the bomb; he was murdered in a separate incident as he rode on the front handlebars of a friend's bike, shot twice in the head by another teenager. The murderer was convicted of the crime but released six months later.

A thoughtful journey through that museum shows all the signs that people had ascended to the throne and taken wrongful authority. A racial slur shouted loudly or whispered quietly was a word of ridicule. People on all sides of the Civil Rights movement were anxious that their way of life would be destroyed. Politicians unknowingly preached relativism as they demanded outside agitators to stay out of their affairs, insisting what was good in the North wasn't good in the South. Many people stood cloaked in the garb of religiosity while inwardly their hearts were far from Him.

It's easy to see these actions and call them sin. But the Bible has a sober indictment. It says that we are all—the religious and the irreligious—sinners. Quoting Isaiah, Jesus called out the Pharisees saying, "These people honor Me with their lips, but their heart is far from Me" (Matthew 15:8).

I have to stop thinking, *They are sinners,* and realize that I am a sinner. I have to see myself as dust.

Yet that's not the whole story. The Bible says we are gold to God, unique among all His creation. However, sin has destroyed our value. The story of the Bible tells us how He is giving us back our value, turning dust into gold.

It's a story of redemption. It begins with life. God gave us life—where else could it possibly come from? Our life is meant to be lived loving God, in close relationship with Him. Instead, we ignore that He gave our life to us.

My dad gave me a car when I turned 16 years old—a 1975 Datsun 280z. When it was new, this car was nicknamed the "poor man's Porsche." Twenty years later, it had lost much of its mystique. Originally red, it had faded to a burnt orange. The engine didn't purr like a lion; it roared like a lawn mower. It had a sunroof, but sometimes it leaked. Despite all this, I liked this car. I was grateful that my dad had given it to me. Loving my dad meant no matter how far I traveled, I would drive that car back to him.

I suppose when I turned 18 I could have taken that car and left. After all, it was mine, or so I thought. The truth was my dad's name was on the title. Running away with the car would have made me a thief.

In the Bronx I have experience with thieves. Not too long ago I was visiting a teen boy in the hospital after he was sliced with a box cutter. I left my bike locked to a post near the street. When I returned, my seat post and bike seat were gone.

It's not uncommon in our neighborhood to be approached by panhandlers with goods for sale. Those goods are normally stolen—stolen to sell in order to get their next fix. Imagine if one of those men approached me with my seat post and bike seat. He would have in his hands something that was mine that he took from me. In that moment I had several choices: (1) to call the cops; (2) to punch him in the face and take my goods back; (3) to ignore him; and (4) to buy my bike parts back.

The choice made would be based on how valuable the items were to me and my disdain, or love, for the thief.

If the stolen items didn't have much worth to me, I would probably just ignore the whole situation. If the goods were valuable to me but I didn't see much worth in the thief, then I might call the cops or physically accost the man. If I love both the stolen item and the culprit, I would offer to buy it back. This would not only show my value of the stolen good but also my love for the thief.

This scenario is hypothetical. So was the one with my dad and my car. The true, eternal reality isn't hypothetical.

God gave us life. Life in its fullest is found in relationship with Him. However, we take that life and live it separate from Him. We take the car and run. We wreck the car. We do so many things that are destructive to our lives. Life doesn't appear to have much value when we are finished with it.

At the end of life, the Giver of life, being honest, has to call us what we are: thieves. He could ignore this fact and give us each another life, but being just, that's not in His nature. Besides, if He values life, why would He give us another one when we destroyed the first? Therefore,

He has to tell us to give up the keys, to turn in the car. The ride is over. Death is the end of every joy ride.

God values the life He gives us. But He also values us! God's value for life and His love for us meet at the Cross. We took life. Someone must pay it back. On the Cross, Jesus paid His life. This wasn't just any life. If He was merely a perfect human, then His death would have paid the price for one life. But because He is God, the source and wellspring of all life, His death was sufficient for all of us. He paid back for everyone what we ourselves took.

But then He went one step further. He didn't choose number one, two, three, or four from my list of options for responding to an offense. He made choice number five. He paid the price for the stolen item and then said, "Here, you can have it back. Not the life that you took, though, but an even better one!"

Standing on my own pedestal, it was hard to understand or want the life Jesus offered me because I saw myself as gold. But God was going to change my thinking. He was going to smash my idol. Nothing would be left but dust. But God makes beautiful things out of dust!

CHAPTER

12

DAY OF RECKONING

After my visit to the Civil Rights museum, a friend and I were walking through Kelly Ingram Park. My friend said something that caused me to think: "I don't understand how people could justify what they did."

Justification is a word that means to make right something that is wrong. As human beings, we always try to find reasons for the wrong we do.

The horrific actions on display in the Civil Rights museum were justified by religion, anxiety, relativism, and ridicule—all signs those that committed them had ascended to their pedestals and taken the place of God. They took control. They took authority. Control and authority unbalanced by holiness and grace are a devastating combination.

Most the time people don't ascend to this pedestal in one giant step. The New York City landscape is filled with huge skyscrapers. They aren't built all at once. They are built floor by floor, from the ground up ascending into the sky. So too are our pedestals. They are built piece by piece, layer by layer. We elevate ourselves bit by bit.

The mindsets that justified these appalling, hateful actions—not just from this era of our history but across world history—weren't even necessarily intentional.

I find that to be true in my life. I wasn't intentionally a Pharisee. I wasn't intentionally ascending to the pedestal. I wasn't scheming to have the world worship me. This was and is a part of my nature as a human being.

My visit to the museum was part of a 4,500 mile journey that began in New York. I rented a car, traveled to Indiana, Missouri, Alabama, Florida, and back to New York City. My mom joined me for much of that journey.

My cruise control was set on the speed limit the whole trip, until my drive from Birmingham to North Carolina. On that leg of the journey, I was looking forward to visiting a friend and mentor, so I decided to up my speed to 74 miles per hour. I justified my choice thinking, *I'll have more time to visit with my friend.*

As I crossed the border of South Carolina into North Carolina, entertained by music from Broadway's *Aladdin* and less aware because of a conversation with my mom, my body tingled when I looked in my rearview mirror to see a police officer. On the side of the road, he informed me I was going 74 miles per hour—in a construction zone!

He asked, "Is there a reason you were going so fast?"

I replied honestly, "I was talking to my mom and listening to good music. I wasn't as aware as I should have been."

I knew I was guilty.

I had two reasons for breaking the law. First, I justified my choice to go four miles per hour over the speed limit by the desire to spend more time with a friend.

Second, I simply was unaware the speed limit had changed from 70 to 55 miles per hour.

Living unaware of the truth doesn't exempt us from accountability. As I watched the police officer in my rearview mirror, I was hoping I would get off with a warning. If he only knew how I felt, the anguish of a Goody Two-shoes getting in trouble, he would certainly know that I had paid sufficient price.

That's not how he saw it. He gave me a piece of paper.

I thought, *OK, I deserve this. I'll pay the fine.*

But his next words sent a rush of warmth to my face, "This is a summons. You have to appear in court in Gaston County on October 20."

"What?!"

I asked a few questions, but it was clear I had ahead of me a day of reckoning when I would have to account for my actions.

From the moment I received a summons to appear in court, I felt dread. My mind raced with possibilities. Being a pastor in the Bronx, I have often counseled others in much more serious predicaments. My advice to myself was the same I have given them.

"Learn a lesson and move on."

But I couldn't let it go. I kept dwelling on the matter. My mind was like a pit-bull with a chew toy. It was fixed on the situation.

I was anxious. I was fearful of destruction!

Everything seemed to be a harsh reminder of my "criminal action": the news had a story of a celebrity arrested driving under the influence, and I got a phone call from someone in Rikers—both in my mind foreshadowed my doom!

I wasn't put at ease until I was able to talk with an attorney in North Carolina. I wouldn't have to go and appear before the court. He would stand in my place. He worked out a deal with the assistant district attorney to reduce the charge from "speeding in a work zone," to an "improper use of equipment." This charge meant less consequence—no points on my license or for my insurance. I still had to pay a $288 fine, pay my lawyer $100, and take an online driving course.

What a relief! What a lesson! This wasn't a lesson in driving or speeding, although I will think twice before driving four miles per hour over the speed limit again. This was instead a lesson about sin, humanity, and God's eternal work.

God helped me see this experience upside down.

God has given us the law. That law is meant for our protection and for the protection of others. Its basis is love. When we break it, we aren't acting in love. Such unloving acts are a natural consequence from standing on our own pedestals, thinking only of ourselves.

The Bible calls this sin. There is no justification for sin. Justification tries to make right something that is wrong. Bigotry, prejudice, murder, and hatred have been justified across history by people standing on pedestals as idols in their own kingdoms.

Being unaware of sin doesn't excuse us. At the same time knowledge of sin, regret for sin, shame from sin, or depression from sin doesn't exempt us from the coming judgment. Only One who stands in my place can do so: Jesus.

He doesn't stand in my place like a lawyer. The lawyer representing me wasn't willing to pay my price. He wasn't willing to take the points on his license or pay the money. Besides, he wasn't qualified. He was a lawbreaker himself. The judge probably was too. At some point they themselves have driven too fast.

On the Day of Judgment for sin, Jesus will stand in my place, willing and qualified. Willing because He loves me. Qualified because He was blameless.

In the Book of Ephesians, we find Paul's summation of the gospel: "But now in Christ Jesus, you were far away have been brought near by the blood of the Messiah" (Ephesians 2:13). Jesus' death brings all sinners—the moral and the immoral, the religious and the irreligious—near to God.

Jesus was the Author becoming like us, entirely human, yet perfectly divine. His death meant one who was entirely right was wronged so that I, entirely wrong, could be made right. I could be justified.

Sin is only justified through faith in Jesus as the one who makes us right. We must see Him as our Savior. To see Jesus as our Savior, we must first see ourselves as sinners.

WEED-SMOKING PASTOR

As a pastor, I frequently visit people in prison. Those trips are rarely fun. Visiting Rikers Island, the primary jail of New York City, involves waking up at four in the morning, taking a subway, a bus, waiting at many different checkpoints, and submitting to several thorough searches. It takes all day.

On one such visit, I was randomly selected to have my hands swabbed and tested for chemical agents. The experience is similar to the type of screening one receives at an airport. A swab attached to a wand is rubbed over both sides of a person's hands. The swab is then placed in a machine.

That morning, I had already watched prison guards perform this procedure on several other fellow visitors. No alarms sounded; no chemical agents were found.

My story was different.

The machine chirped over the muted conversations of visitors: *Beep. Beep. Beep.*

Without making eye contact the guard said, "Go wash your hands."

Puzzled, I went to the restroom, washed my hands, and returned.

The guard swabbed them again and then placed the swab in the machine.

Beep. Beep. Beep.

"Try washing them again."

I repeated the process and again. *Beep. Beep. Beep.*

Finally looking at me, the guard said, "You only get three tries."

I pleaded, "The machine must be mistaken. I am a pastor coming to visit someone from my church. What does it say is on my hands, anyway?"

"THC—marijuana," he said, marking in a logbook.

I imagined what he was thinking, *A weed-smoking pastor?!*

He confirmed my suspicion when he said, "We don't care what you do in your free time, but you won't be allowed a contact visit today."

In other words, I would only be able to see the inmate on the other side of a glass wall.

I assured him defensively, "I don't smoke weed, but a lot of people in my apartment building do!"

Sometimes I chuckle about the places I go. I find myself in places I never imagined I would be. Visiting prisons, going to court, and walking the streets of the Bronx late at night are all unlikely scenarios for a small-town boy from Missouri.

Earlier in my life, ridicule dominated my mind. I would look at people in these places and think, *They're getting what they deserve!*

God has changed my way of thinking. He has used these people to help me see others differently and, more importantly, see myself differently.

In my experience, perspective yields compassion. Certainly being able to see a little through another person's eyes helps us withhold judgment. Even more, perspective about ourselves yields compassion.

On a cool summer evening in the South Bronx, I walked onto the stoop of my apartment building with my dog, Proof. Looking up the block, I saw the familiar red-and-blue flashes of emergency vehicles. Curious, I walked with Proof up the block.

Yellow crime-scene tape blocked off a street, and the block was covered with men and women in blue. Along with these officers were men and women in suits, police detectives, collecting evidence and trying to piece together the events surrounding yet another shooting in our neighborhood.

Returning home, I wondered if someone I knew was involved. Later that evening I got a call. A familiar voice asked me to come to the hospital.

I rode my blue bike down the dark city streets smattered with orange from the city lights above. It was about midnight. The ride was short, only about ten minutes. I locked my bike to the fence outside the hospital and hoped it would be there when I returned. The person in admissions helped me determine my destination. I took the elevator to the sixth floor and made my way through the familiar maze of corridors.

As I walked onto sixth floor, I heard someone screaming. I looked at the numbers next to the door of each room, and searched for 628.

620. 621. 622. 623. 624.

I was walking toward the screaming. I knew the voice.

625. 626. 627. 628.

I walked into the room and saw a church member, a friend, a brother in total agony. All I could do was sit next to him and hold his hand, a hand that clenched mine.

His leg had been broken. The same leg also had two bullet holes in it from a shooting two weeks earlier.

The shots fired earlier that night were aimed at him but didn't hit him. When gunfire rang out, everyone fled, including him. Cops on the scene didn't know who had shot the gun. Chasing my friend down, the police officer hit him with his car, and another officer tackled him to the ground. In the commotion, my friend's leg was not just fractured but broken in half. The young man sat handcuffed outside the elevator of his apartment for two hours before receiving medical treatment.

I didn't know the whole story when I walked in the room. All I knew was my friend was in pain.

A nurse entered the room.

I sat with my friend's hand in my hand and listened to the nurse ask him questions.

"Did you learn your lesson? What's it going to take for you to figure things out? It's the same, day after day."

Each one of the nurse's comments was like another shot fired at my friend. As I listened, I got angry.

I finally interrupted the barrage and said, "He's not a thug! Don't treat him like one!"

This nurse thought he had my friend figured out. He immediately judged him as a thug.

I have to admit, my friend looked the part and had the battle scars to prove it.

But there was so much this nurse didn't know about my friend. The nurse had never seen this young gentleman respectfully hold the door open for my mother. He had never seen this older brother fix his little sister's bike in the courtyard of their building. He had never seen this son help his mom carry in the groceries. He never saw this friend jump while watching a scary movie in a theater. He had never prayed with this church member.

The nurse had no compassion because his perspective was so limited.

His perspective of me was limited as well. Throughout the exam the nurse's eyes darted back and forth from me to his patient. I felt like I could read his mind. It seemed he was thinking, *Who's this guy? Why is he here? The two of them couldn't be more different.*

By this point in my life, though, God had already used my friend and many others to help me see myself differently.

I had answered the question Ariel helped me to ask years before this night in Chicago. The question, *What is the gospel?*

Many people have answered this question in different ways. One theologian summed up the gospel with three words: "God saves sinners." My life and experience with ministry has led me to add two words to that summation: "God saves sinners like me!"

Sitting next to my friend while he was in his hospital bed, I knew I was no different from him. He was a sinner. I was a sinner. Our sins may look different on the outside, but to God the outside isn't what matters. Only by God's grace my sins hadn't led to horrific consequences in my own life.

Also by God's grace I was saved. God wrote that story in my life, just as He was writing that story in my friend's life. With Him as the Author, I have no reason to boast, yet instead sat humbly, compassionately next to my friend as he clenched my hand pleading for relief from the pain.

CHAPTER

14

OPEN THEM ALL THE WAY

Several years after Ariel's confession of faith in Jesus, he told me, "I'm here. I've made it out. For those kids coming from a tough place, I want to open their eyes a little so they can see for themselves, and maybe when they start seeing, they can open them all the way."

Ariel helped me open my eyes a little. My Author has been doing that through him and others. The more I see, the wider I want them open.

Seeing can be a struggle. So often we sit like the cave dwellers in Plato's allegory of the cave. Bound and shackled, facing the interior of a cave, the prisoners watched the shadows on the rock of people who passed by a fire behind them. As people walked by, the cave-dwellers mistakenly thought their words were the sound of the shadows. They thought the shadows were real. It's no wonder they formed this conclusion. They had never seen the light; they didn't have any basis of knowing reality.

At some point one prisoner gets free. Turning and walking toward the fire, at first the light hurts his eyes. Eventually though, the pain gives way to clearer vision, and he realizes what he had experienced his whole life wasn't real.

Upon exiting the cave, his pain only intensifies. The light of the sun was so much brighter than the fire. Slowly his eyes adjust once again, and he is able to see the true reality from a never-ending source of light.

Plato's tale is a good story. It's a lot like our Author's.

We sit, bound like the cave dwellers, mistakenly thinking that all we experience in this life is real. Why would we think otherwise? That changes, though, when we read the story of one who came from outside the cave. His life told plainly of the world outside our cave. Then His death and new life broke the chains that imprison us.

The Author wants us to know this story so that we will leave the cave. We may not want to leave because we find pleasure in the lives we have scavenged for ourselves in the cave. We may not be able to leave because of the many layers of gold we have forged on the idol of ourselves. We don't fit through the door.

Our only hope is the Author Himself. Like a dawning of the sun revealing the true nature of what we see in the dark, He must show us who we really are. He must take His hammer and smash the idol we build of our self.

That's what God did in my life. He used people to change the way I think, but most of all He used sin. Through seeing my sin, God smashed the idol I made of myself. For so many years, there was no room for Him on the pedestal because I was there.

Over many years, my Creator's love became apparent. I understood the depths of His love because I understood the depths of my sin.

Knowing my sin helped me have a new way of thinking. Like the cave dweller, I view all of life differently, especially my sin. No longer do my thoughts linger on the hypocrisy of my sin. Instead, I think, *I don't have to be who I used to be. I can change. I can do something right now in this moment that I have never done before!*

Ultimately, understanding the depths of our sin is a prerequisite to eternal joy. One might think that such awareness would be the cause for depression.

This is upside down from the eternal truth.

Chapter 14

The more I realize my sin, the more I elevate Jesus and want to be more like Him. The more I realize my sin, the more I understand Jesus' message.

This is what He said: "The kingdom of God, has come near . . ." (Mark 1:15). In other words, "God is sitting on the throne, not you."

"Repent . . ." Change your thinking.

"Believe . . ." Have faith. Trust God not yourself.

"In the good news!" The bad news: you're a sinner. The good news: I can bring all—the moral and immoral, the religious and the irreligious—near to God. I can save sinners like you!

SICKNESS

August 27, 2012

"We found a mass. It looks like testicular cancer."

My cancer was gone, gone due to the attention and expertise of top-notch medical care. However, the Great Physician
did so much more than just heal me physically.

CHAPTER 15

CANCEROUS JOY

The Great Physician used sickness in my life to bring more than just physical healing. Through my journey, I witnessed firsthand that He was the writer of my story, even the chapter that involved cancer. The name of that chapter was *Cancerous Joy*.

Cancerous joy.

A quick Internet search reveals the definition for *cancer* is, "The disease caused by the uncontrolled division of abnormal cells in a part of the body." These are cells that respond in an unexpected manner. They multiply at an accelerated rate.

The definition for *joy* is, "The feeling of great pleasure and happiness."

A combination of the two definitions is, "the uncontrolled feeling of abnormal pleasure and happiness."

Cancerous joy: joy that is unexpected and multiplies at an accelerated rate.

I don't know exactly when it began, just as I don't know when the cancer cells began forming in my body. All I know is both the cells and joy multiplied unexpectedly, at an accelerated rate.

Unlike my cancer, which I didn't know the cause or origin, I knew the source of my joy. It was my faith. My faith was supported by three core truths: (1) God is the Author of my story. He is in control; (2) I didn't choose the road I had traveled, and I couldn't choose the road ahead, but I could choose how I would walk it; and (3) I wanted to walk in a way that glorified God.

Too often sickness and other tough circumstances lead us to other conclusions. Sometimes we conclude God isn't in control. Other times we think He doesn't love us. Then we think Satan or maybe a sin caused a certain problem. We see in the Book of Job that God was in control of what was happening to Job. If we say Satan is the cause of our difficulties, then we are saying our circumstances are outside of God's control. Traversing any of these trails leads to confusion. Sometimes we get so far down the road that we need to return to the beginning and start fresh.

Once, while riding my bike on a rocky trail in the Ozark Mountains of Missouri, I began to feel more and more confused. Having looked at the map posted at the trailhead, as I came to forks in the road, I thought I knew which way to go. As I traveled farther down the path, it made less and less sense, and the trail became more and more difficult. Finally I stopped pedaling, got off my bike, and took a moment to appraise the situation. I realized I was far from where I needed to be. I needed to reverse direction. I eventually got back to the place where I made the wrong turn and corrected my course.

When facing troubling circumstances, one path leads to life, understanding, and even cancerous joy.

The first step on the path to cancerous joy is recognizing that God is the Author of our story and He is in control. He is all-powerful, all-knowing, and entirely good. These eternal realities viewed in light of His abundant love for His creation lead to only one conclusion. He is working good in our lives. He isn't just manipulating things for our good. He is planning things for our good. Yes, there is the adversary. Even he, though, isn't out of the control of the One who is writing the story. Therefore, no weapon he uses against us will be successful.

I saw the Author's deft hand in my story when I arrived at the hospital in St. Louis at the beginning my treatment for testicular cancer.

I parked my car in a parking garage, stepped out and to my surprise heard someone say, "Andrew?!"

I turned around, and there stood a longtime family friend. He reached down (he is very tall, and I'm not) and gave me a big, bearish hug. I knew why he was there. His wife had been fighting cancer for 20 years. Her stomach had recently been removed, and as I suspected, she was at the hospital for follow-up appointments.

He didn't know why I was there, though. After a brief explanation he said, "I'll tell my wife."

As I was signing in at the urology office, I heard the familiar voices of my two friends talking to my mom. I sat with them on the teal, vinyl chairs. We talked. They prayed for me, and his wife embraced me with a hug that felt like the arms of God.

This wasn't coincidence. It wasn't happenstance. God wanted me to see He was in control, so He provided this veteran warrior of cancer to walk me onto the battlefield.

The second step toward joy in the midst of my cancer was a logical conclusion once I realized the first. I am not in control.

I never realized this more than while I was in chemotherapy. I had no control of what was happening in my body. While taking a shower, I looked at my hands and saw huge clumps of hair. I would hiccup uncontrollably, shaking my whole body. This would send acid from my stomach up my esophagus and into my throat. Then I would throw up. Meanwhile, I was constipated. I wanted to go to the bathroom but couldn't.

To combat nausea, my doctor gave me steroids. He warned they might make me feel aggressive. One day following treatment, I was walking a couple blocks to the pharmacy to pick up a prescription. As I walked down the sidewalk, I noticed ahead of me two individuals soliciting signatures for a petition. Clad in hippy garb, the woman with clipboard in one hand raised the other and exclaimed exuberantly, "High five!"

Feeling ill from treatment, I responded, "Not right now."

With a snippety tone she murmured, "It's just a high five."

Something boiled in me. In an instant, condemning thoughts bubbled judging her tone, lack of perspective, and selfishness. I turned, pointed to my gauze-wrapped wrist, and said, "I just had a three-hour IV treatment in my hand, so no, I don't want to give you a high-five!"

At the end of the block, I turned and looked back at her. She had a big smile, her hand raised high, waving to me. I turned the corner shaking my head wondering, *Is this 'roid rage?*

I clearly wasn't in control of my body or mind.

I was on a path I didn't plan or choose. It wasn't a story I would have written for myself. I also knew I couldn't control the road ahead, but I was in control of one thing. I could control how I would walk it.

An overwhelming desire set in to walk the path in a way that glorified God. I knew He would be glorified in my story.

God is honored as we approach current situations with eternity in mind, or in other words, upside down. With this mindset, He is able to accomplish His work both in our lives and through our lives. Another name for this work is ministry. Unexpected circumstances present the greatest opportunity for ministry. And the opportunity for ministry depends on our response.

People respond differently to the same circumstance. The children and teens I work with at our ministry center in the Bronx demonstrated this vividly when they saw my bald head. The night before, my friend had helped me shave my head. I made this choice after seeing piles of hair sticking to my hands in the shower as a result of chemotherapy.

Sitting in the office of our center as kids came in after school, I thought their reactions as they walked by were funny. Eyes enlarged; some stared. Many did a double or even triple-take. One third-grade boy exclaimed with mouth wide open, "Whoa!" The rest of the day he pretended not to look, but his eyes darted back and forth every time I walked by.

Some kids were scared. Others with a look of concern asked, "Why?" One boy fell out of his chair, laughing on the floor. Some were unresponsive, indicating either they didn't notice or didn't care.

A few of the teens said, "I think it's cool . . . No really, I'm not joking."

Another asked, "Is that from the cancer?"

We all respond to information and circumstances in different ways. Some make judgments, some jump to conclusions without all the information, others sympathize internally by feeling pity. Many respond saying, "I know exactly what you are going through," and begin to speak of their own struggles and woes.

It became commonplace for people to offer solutions in an effort to extend comfort. "You should try eating beets. . . . You shouldn't eat anything spicy. . . . I read a book that says there are natural cures. . . . You'll feel better if you pinch your nose, close your eyes, and spin around five times while singing a song."

Uncomfortable, a lot of people simply avoid the obvious altogether.

A few respond with empathy and compassion.

Compassion is shown through a heart-felt question that is seeking understanding; it's shown through a phone call, note, or letter; it's shown through an individual meeting an unexpressed need. Compassion is shown through prayer—even when the person being prayed for doesn't know. Compassion is shown by laughing with someone. Compassion is shown by giving space when space is needed. Compassion is shown through a hot meal.

Such compassion is evidence of eternity and the work of the Author in a person's life. Everywhere Jesus went, He showed compassion. He stopped to address the physical, mental, emotional, social, and spiritual hurts of friends, family, and strangers. Most of His responses were quite unexpected, responding in a way I would never think to respond, always though, exactly what the person needed.

Jesus' responses weren't merely an outflowing of His eternal, divine nature. He was equally like us; He was human. He knew pain; He knew sorrow; He knew sickness. His unexpected, compassionate responses were the result of living divinely human, living in this world with eternity in mind. This mindset was the outflowing of the relationship He had with his Father, a synergy that is offered to me.

Oh how this brings me joy! I am human like Jesus. My Father desires the same relationship with me. That means I can be Jesus to those around me who hurt physically, mentally, emotionally, socially, and spiritually. Just like Jesus, I can have unexpected responses to unexpected circumstances.

About a week after my first surgery in St. Louis, I returned to the Bronx. A young man saw me hobbling down the street, still sore from surgery and asked, "What happened?"

I told him about my cancer diagnosis.

He told me about his grandfather who recently died of cancer.

He asked, "Aren't you scared?"

Cancerous joy had already taken root in my life. I said, "No. I'm at total peace with what is happening. I trust God."

A few nights later, he approached me on the street while I was walking Proof. He asked me many questions. It was clear He was thinking about life and death.

We went up to my apartment and chatted until one in the morning. He asked, "How are you not scared?"

I told him about my Author's story. My unexpected, joyful response to my unexpected circumstance raised questions in His mind.

This young man didn't find His story in the pages of our Author's story that night, but I was able to glorify God through my unexpected response.

Cancerous joy can be infectious. Although cancer doesn't spread from person to person, cancerous joy does. Great struggle presents us with great opportunities to help others see differently.

At the beginning of my treatment, I visited with a young man I knew from our ministry center. After catching up on his life, I told him I had been diagnosed with cancer. He was stunned. I shared with him the whole story as well as what I anticipated to be the journey ahead.

Confused, he said, "I don't get it, Andrew. You are a pastor. You're a good person. You don't do anything bad."

He was well down the road of believing that God didn't love him. He thought God was spiteful and vengeful. He didn't see God as the Author, totally in control.

I understood why he thought this way. I knew his backstory. When he was young, his little brother was murdered by his father. I knew this young man carried a sense of blame. His mom had angrily told him many times, "If you hadn't gone to Burger King . . ." She blamed him for her baby's death.

This knowledge motivated my response as I replied, "This didn't happen to me because I did something wrong just as your brother didn't die because you did something wrong."

A nearly visible weight was lifted as he asked, "You mean it wasn't my fault?"

God can work through our lives as we experience sickness. Ultimately our unexpected response to unexpected circumstances impacts others. It glorifies God.

CHAPTER

16   CUT IT OFF

Cancer not only taught me about joy, it also taught me more about sin. Sin is a cancer of the soul. Diagnosing and treating this more devastating disease of the spirit is the same as diagnosing and treating our bodies.

New York is full of eccentric people. One grows accustomed to seeing oddities. Times Square has the Naked Cowboy. I have chuckled at a man in Union Square joyously dancing back and forth wearing only green briefs. Not as amusing was a man in a subway station hurling his arms and contorting his body to the sound of music in a manner I think he intended to be interpretive dance. He was wearing only a pink-and-black negligee.

Such flamboyant immodesty is unfathomable to me. As a teen, I was nervous changing in the locker room. Afraid of judgment, I wanted to keep my hidden parts hidden.

Even as a 30-year-old being examined by my doctor-friend, I was nervous about dropping my pants. I was hoping my friend would skip that part. My anticipation of his thoroughness couldn't be avoided as he donned a pair of sterile gloves.

Honestly, I had noticed months before what he noticed in that moment. My testicle was enlarged. I ignored that fact. I continued with life as usual, occasionally wondering if my enlarged testicle was cause for alarm but mostly minimizing and rationalizing this fact away.

Avoiding the truth doesn't change the truth.

For years I had done the same thing with sin. I knew I had a problem, but I ignored it. As a Pharisee, a master of religion, I was outwardly self-controlled. The outside of the cup and dish were clean, but inside I was full of greed and self-indulgence (Matthew 23:25). Secret sin ravaged my life privately and internally. Lust and pornography were a daily struggle. The cycle was consistent. Access fed curiosity. Curiosity led to exploration. Exploration gave way to desire. Desire fueled fantasy. Fantasy brought pleasure. Pleasure was followed by guilt. Guilt provoked "repentance." But like a dog returned to his vomit, I would return to my sin (Proverbs 26:11). The same thoughts would return, unchanged.

Repentance is insincere and ineffective without authenticity. As long as sin stays in the dark, it will never be seen for what it truly is and we will never acknowledge the consequence.

What is the consequence of sin? Sin destroys our connection to eternity. It kills us. Just like the cancer in my body, it's not a matter of if; it's a matter of when. What began in my testicle had already made its way to my abdomen. It was doubling in size every ten days. It wouldn't be long before it was in my lungs and brain. If the truth of my enlarged testicle was never acknowledged, if I continued to excuse, minimize, and rationalize it away, I was dead.

Sin is no different. It spreads like a cancer while we excuse, minimize, and rationalize it away. Sin destroys our connection to eternity. Our souls last forever; our bodies don't. God's Word tells us that we are dead in our sins. It's not a matter of if, but when.

That's why Jesus took sin so seriously. He said, "If your right eye causes you to sin, gouge it out and throw it away . . . And if your right hand causes you to sin, cut it off and throw it away" (Matthew 5:29–30).

He then explained why such drastic action is worth the sacrifice, "For it is better that you lose one of the parts of your body than for your whole body to go into hell" (v. 30). If our flesh causes us to sin, it's entirely worth any extreme action to secure heaven, the ultimate reward.

However, we don't take sin this seriously. We not only minimize and rationalize our sin, we do the same with Jesus' words. We call them metaphorical. Yet for me, God wrote this story literally.

The part of my body that caused me to sin was cut off! Remember Skipper, my dog who was neutered? My innocent, naïve concern was justified!

The truth is that surgery alone can't change our thinking. Ultimately the problem is in our mind. Therefore, the first step to solving our sin is acknowledging it. However, another step is required.

Once I was diagnosed with cancer, I needed help to treat it. Even if I had mutilated the part of my body where the sin had originated, the disease wouldn't have been removed. The cancer was rapidly progressing across my entire body.

Time and time again, I had to confess my problem to others. I had to tell doctors my problem and allow them to examine me. I could have never solved my cancer-problem without their help. Authentically confessing our struggle with sin to those we trust may seem upside down, but it is the path to healing for our soul.

Ultimately, the Bible says to confess our sin to God (1 John 1:9). After all, Jesus said, "Those who are well don't need a doctor, but the sick do need one. I didn't come to call the righteous, but sinners" (Mark 2:17). Jesus is the physician of our soul. He knows exactly what to do.

Treating sin involves both acknowledging and confessing. But acknowledging and confessing alone don't glorify God. A third step is necessary.

I am not shy to praise my doctors for healing my cancer. I was blessed with amazing medical care all along the way. Nevertheless, if I didn't follow their advice by doing what they said, I likely would not have been healed.

Once the Physician tells us what to do, He will only get the glory if we do it.

It's no mystery what the Physician tells us to do. It's spoken plainly in His Word. Sometimes it looks upside down to us, so it's easy to rationalize another way, to find reasons to come to another conclusion.

This happened to me before I started chemotherapy. I had a decision to make. The chemicals in my body would decrease my potential fertility, and the surgery that followed would destroy it. Therefore, my doctors advised me to bank sperm in case I married and wanted to conceive a child someday.

God's Word seemed to provide a clear answer to this concern. It says, "Don't worry about tomorrow, because tomorrow will worry about itself. Each day has enough trouble of its own" (Matthew 6:34).

It says, "Defend the rights of the fatherless" (Isaiah 1:17). God is a "father to the fatherless" (Psalm 68:5). We should be the same. Sometimes biological fatherhood can hinder our ability to obey this command.

It says, "Run from sexual immorality" (1 Corinthians 6:18). Knowing the secret, sinful, struggle I had combatted, the process of sperm banking didn't seem like something that would be God-honoring.

Throughout the Bible God makes possible the impossible. Yet, we shouldn't be amazed by His miracles; amazement is symptomatic of disbelief. Amazement shows we don't trust He is writing a story in which He is entirely in control. The events that He is writing don't have to make sense; He's not limited to the logical. Abnormal to us is normal for God. He is miraculous.

His Word is full of those types of miraculous stories. Abraham was told that he would have a son. When he reached one hundred years of age, it seemed impossible. However with an all-powerful Creator, nothing is impossible. Abraham had a son.

As I faced my decision to bank sperm, I thought, *Perhaps my Author will write a story similar to Abraham's in my life.*

With God's Word in mind, I concluded sperm banking was not for me.

But then I reconsidered. I listened to other people's perspectives. I considered my options. I tried to be logical.

I researched into a nonprofit organization that would provide financial assistance. I began to think it would be wise to preserve future choice, both for me and for any potential spouse. Together we could one day make that reproductive decision.

I made an appointment for ten o'clock one morning. From the moment I made the appointment, I felt unsettled. The peace that had existed a few days before was now replaced with anxiety. I spent an hour trying to rationalize my decision. At nine o'clock I was at a fork in the road. I either had to head to the subway to meet my appointment, or call and cancel it. An inaudible voice resounded in my soul saying, "I told you the way, now walk it."

I remembered what God said through the prophet Isaiah, "And whenever you turn to the right or to the left, your ears will hear this command behind you: 'This is the way. Walk in it'" (Isaiah 30:21).

I cancelled the appointment.

I was confident, that whatever happened in my life—sin or sickness, then, now, or later—He was writing my story.

He could be glorified by this story—both my story of cancer and my story of sin. All I needed to do was authentically acknowledge the problem, vulnerably confess it to others, listen to the physicians, and do what they said.

THE GREAT PHYSICIAN

Sometimes, like my cancer, we don't know the cause of our sickness. Other times, the cause is readily apparent. Sometimes it is obvious to others, even when it isn't obvious to us.

I'm often asked, "How did your dog, Proof, respond to your cancer?" People expect my super-dog with her supernatural powers to have had some amazing response. Of course there are many stories of dogs that do such amazing things. Medic-alert dogs alert people to seizures, high blood sugar, and low blood sugar. I've even heard of dogs that can sniff out cancer.

That's not Proof! She has a hard time sniffing out a ball that is hidden a few feet from her!

Honestly, I didn't notice any difference in her while I was sick. However, she has helped me better understand sickness and the work of the Physician to heal us.

Proof is a remarkable dog, but sometimes she does things that are offensive to me. She mostly offends me by the things she eats. The only food she is permitted is the food I give her, and I give her plenty of it. I feed her in the morning and at night. Her plumpness shows that she is well cared for. Nevertheless, if she knows I'm not watching, she will root around on the ground, scavenging for "food" in its most disgusting forms! (Yeah, go ahead and tell me she's smart!)

The things she eats off the filthy city sidewalks are not only gross to me, but they make her sick. Some could even cause her death.

Therefore, when I catch her doing things that offend me and hurt her, I correct her. There are three methods I was taught in the training program that trained both her and me: (1) I say, "No," with a growly tone; (2) I pull the leash connected to the choke-collar—it doesn't hurt her, just gets her attention; and (3) in extreme cases, I give her an "alpha roll." I flip her over on her back, pinning her to the ground until her body goes limp.

I don't do these things because I am mean. I do them because I love her. I demonstrate my power because I know things she doesn't know. I know her offensive behavior will hurt her.

She doesn't think about that. She only thinks about the short-term pleasure it gives her without much thought for the delayed consequence. If I could, maybe I would become a dog like so that I could tell her what she could do to honor me and have the best dog life possible. Knowing that she is a dog though, I know that unless something is changed, she will continue to do the things dogs do.

So, what if I could become a dog, and never do those things that result in death. What if then I allowed my father to sternly pull my collar, flip me over, and say, "No!" All so that in observing me, she wouldn't have to have the same consequence.

If I received those consequences on her behalf, I would want her to have a relationship with me. I would want her to understand me and then we could truly communicate with each other.

In that relationship she would have freedom and responsibility. She would go places where ordinary dogs could never go. She would still face discipline for those silly things she does, but she would be protected from the ultimate consequences.

To be honest, even if I could become like her, I don't know if I love her enough to become a dog.

The Author of our story did.

We aren't much different. Proverbs 26:11 says, "Like a dog returns to its vomit, so a fool repeats his foolishness." Furthermore, God isn't less revolted by my sin than I am by Proof's disgusting behavior. Revelation 3:16 says our behavior, our sin, our religious mediocrity makes God sick: "So, because you are lukewarm, and neither hot nor cold, I am going to vomit you out of my mouth."

The Great Physician knew it would take an extreme act to treat our sickness. He knew that, left on our own, we would be as clueless and impotent as Proof to do anything about what is so obviously killing us.

He loves us abundantly, so His word became flesh in Jesus. He became like us to teach us about His Father and His Father's kingdom. Many around Him, like us, continued to focus on their own kingdoms. Seeking their own pleasure, they failed to see the eternal truth. Their schemes resulted in His torture, disgrace, and execution. At least that was their perspective.

The eternal perspective is different.

The eternal perspective looks upside down to us. What seemed to be bad news was good news. What seemed to be death was life. What seemed to be humiliation was glorification.

Imagine if my love for Proof caused me to push her away from an oncoming car, and instead I took the hit. If another dog did that, it would be remarkable, but it wouldn't be nearly as meaningful as me sacrificing my life.

If Jesus was just a human sacrifice, it would be remarkable but ultimately wouldn't mean much. The only way it matters is if Jesus was Himself the Author of the story. Jesus' crucifixion on the Cross is the clearest evidence of our Author's love for us. He, different from us, with all authority, knowledge, and power, loved us enough to become like us, teach us, and save us from the consequences of temporary, short-term living.

Jesus' crucifixion is the extreme act of the Great Physician. A Physician who didn't merely tell us what to do, but took our place. I was blessed to have great doctors administer well-researched, experienced, medical care. However, not one of them sat next to me with

IV in arm as poison pumped through their body. My surgeon didn't sit next to me on the operating table allowing himself to be cut in half. Jesus did.

CHAPTER

18 HEALTH=SEEPS

Experiencing sickness causes one to think more about health. Health is a person's state of well-being. Although most people know there is more to health than just our bodies, we give the greatest attention to them by far.

Trillions of dollars are spent every year to promote good physical health. Science tells us what to eat, how to exercise, and how to sleep. Now there are apps to track all these aspects of health in detail.

Health and well-being are also important in God's Word. A colleague of mine in the city runs a sister ministry in Brooklyn. He has founded practices for healthy living based on the life of Elijah. Elijah was on the run after killing all of Ahab's prophets. He was afraid and would rather face death than those that pursued him. When we would rather die than live, we are not in a healthy state of being.

God brought Elijah back to health. The story can be found in 1 Kings 19. First, Elijah slept. Then Elijah ate. He ate again. Then he walked for forty days and forty nights. He found a cave and isolated himself from the world. God met him there.

My colleague uses Elijah's example to describe healthy practices with the acronym SEEP: sleep, eat, exercise, and pray.

Sleep can be a catch-22. Without sleep we aren't healthy. If we aren't healthy, we often can't sleep. During chemotherapy when my body would spasm with hiccups, I would lie in bed, miserable, wanting only to sleep.

But simply wanting sleep doesn't solve the problem, Sometimes the problem is physical.

My mother struggled for years with sleep until she got a CPAP machine. It's amazing how much better she felt with the assistance of that ventilation device. But sometimes treating sleep problems as only physical doesn't always solve the problem. In fact, it can create more problems.

As a pastor in the Bronx, I come across many individuals with addictions. One of those individuals was addicted to sleep medication. It was obtained legally through a therapist and psychiatrist. This person had never met the psychiatrist; instead, the doctor just wrote the prescriptions. This person would not only take the meds at night but frequently throughout the day, creating a numbed reality which was often unpleasant.

God's Word says we should even look at sleep upside down. In Psalm 16 the psalmist finds rest at night. He doesn't sleep well because all in his life is well. In fact he is in need of refuge. He has nothing good in his life besides God.

The psalmist's rest comes from seeing the world upside down, focusing on eternity rather than his immediate circumstance. He says, "I will praise the Lord who counsels me—even at night my conscience instructs me. I will keep the Lord in mind always. Because He is at my right hand, I will not be shaken" (Psalm 16:7–8).

At night when he can't sleep, he praises God. He keeps God in mind rather than the barrage of worries like those that often flood our minds. Being in God's presence, living with the end in mind, gives the psalmist abundant joy.

Eating is important to health as well. Of course good health isn't just about eating, but eating well. I'm reminded of the words of the ancient Greek physician, Hippocrates, "Let food be thy medicine and medicine be thy food." He lived about five hundred years after Elijah.

Hippocrates imagined one day all medical concerns would be treated with nutrition. Boy, was he wrong!

Following my surgery, the one that nearly cut me in half, I had to be on a low-fat diet for a month. The lipids in fat would cause fluid to build up in my abdomen and ultimately lead to infection. I was limited to five grams of fat a day. Of course my nature was to exceed expectations, so I cut fat out altogether.

To achieve this, I had to think about what I ate. I had to read labels and calculate nutritional data. For most of my life, I hadn't thought much about what I ate. If I wanted it, I ate it. But during that month, I had to think about what I ate. I mainly ate fruits, vegetables, and grain. That month recalibrated my system. Following that diet, I no longer wanted things I craved before.

I now eat differently; I eat *thinkingly*. Although so much of our lives is spent in self-preservation, when it comes to things we eat, it's not always best to do what comes naturally. Our cravings can destroy life rather than preserve it.

The same is true with exercise. Exercise can cause pain. Our natural inclination is to avoid pain. We avoid it because we first associate pain as life threatening. When our well-being is infringed upon, the body screams to get our attention so we will react and change the circumstance causing the pain.

Pain can also be a sign of life. Immediately after my surgery I had a PCA, a machine with a button that, when pushed, administers pain medication. These medications either deaden nerves or limit the brain's receptors to pick up the signals these nerves are sending. The pain I was feeling was a sign that I was alive, not dead. Sometimes my incision would tingle. This was my body healing.

Wisdom is knowing whether our pain is life-threatening or life-promoting. If the pain is life-threatening, we certainly need to do something to change our circumstances. If we do not respond to the life-threatening pain, we may be in grave danger.

If the pain is life-promoting, then we need to do something that feels upside down—not shy away from the pain.

As I said earlier, I started exercising after my surgery. I rarely wanted to exercise, but never once did I regret it. Yes, my body was sore and I felt pain. But that pain was life-promoting.

With my new eating and exercise practices, I lost almost 60 pounds. I was healthier than I had ever been in my life—certainly upside down to what we normally think is the outcome of cancer.

The *P* in SEEPS stands for prayer. Prayer is one means by which we grow in our knowledge of God. It is the means by which we develop our eternal lenses.

After my chemotherapy, my mom came to the city to visit. Being the holiday season, we attended the Rockettes Christmas Spectacular at Radio City Music Hall. Because of long bathroom lines we were a little late to arrive in the theater. The show was already well in motion as we walked down the aisle. A video was playing on a large screen. The video was blurry and unfocused. Once I sat down though, I put on the 3D lenses received from an usher. It was quite spectacular from that moment forward.

Prayer brings the spiritual reality into focus. Life can seem blurry without the spiritual lens of prayer.

Jesus taught us to how to pray. When I read His teaching, I think He taught us to pray upside down!

Consider His model prayer found in Matthew 6:9–13:

> *Therefore, you should pray like this: Our Father in heaven, Your name be honored as holy. Your kingdom come. Your will be done on earth as it is in heaven. Give us today our daily bread. And forgive us our debts, as we also have forgiven our debtors. And do not bring us into temptation, but deliver us from the evil one. [For Yours is the kingdom and the power and the glory forever. Amen.]*

Meditating on each word of this model prayer has enriched my prayer life.

Our: It's not just *me*. There's an *us*. I am part of a family of believers.

Father: I am a child of God. That makes Jesus my brother. A child has rights and responsibilities, privileges and priorities.

In heaven: What is heaven really like? I can only imagine . . . but never fail to imagine!

Your name be honored as holy: How can my life promote God's name? When I die, Jesus' name will be the only name that matters to me.

Your kingdom come. Your will be done on earth as it is in heaven: Not my will be done. God's will. What is His will? Sometimes our wills have to be weakened in order to know His will.

Give us today our daily bread: I once heard a sermon by John Piper that observed from John 6, "Jesus didn't come to give you bread but to be your bread." So rather than praying for my temporary, time-bound, physical needs be met, I should pray for my spiritual needs to be met.

And forgive us our debts as we also have forgiven our debtors: The patience God has shown to me should be reflected in the patience I show others.

Do not bring us into temptation, but deliver us from the evil one: Honestly, this is a phrase I continue to meditate on. I don't quite understand it. Jesus was led into temptation. Job was led into temptation. I don't understand why Jesus would ask us to pray for something that God doesn't necessarily answer. It's OK that I don't yet understand. I will continue to meditate on this.

For Yours is the kingdom and the power and the glory forever: Anything I build isn't forever. What He is building will last.

Here's an observation that has transformed my life: most of this prayer focuses on the eternal; it focuses on the end. Jesus tells us to pray upside down.

Jesus' example of prayer is not meant to be an event in our day or week. Scripture says, "Pray constantly" (1 Thessalonians 5:17). Prayer is living every moment with the end in mind.

My colleague ends the acronym with prayer—SEEP. I find great value in adding another letter—SEEPS. Elijah took time to get alone. He wasn't working; he was resting. In this time he encountered God; he connected to the eternal. He took time to Sabbath. *S* stands for Sabbath.

Growing up, I never knew the concept of Sabbath; it was the day I went to church, but it was largely still foreign to me. But with the help of good mentors in my life, now I not only understand it, and I can't live without it.

Sabbath is a time not to *do* but instead simply to *be*. It's a time intentionally set apart to refrain from work.

Our ministry in the Bronx structures time for Sabbath. Friday is our Sabbath, and we rarely schedule anything on that day. Sometimes I lock myself in my apartment, not too different from Elijah's cave, and do not emerge until Saturday. Sometimes I explore the city. The key for me is not to do or think in the ways I do the other six days of the week. Sometimes the thinking can be hard!

The Sabbath is restorative for me. Jesus taught this saying, "The Sabbath was made for man and not man for the Sabbath" (Mark 2:27). For me, the proof of this is when I miss the Sabbath. It occasionally happens, sometimes for good reasons, other times for poor reasons. Whatever the reason, I hunger and thirst for this day of rest, especially when it has been intruded upon.

Similar to Sabbath is the habit of creating margins. Margins are intentionally creating time in the day, week, month, and year not to *do*, just to *be*. In the week, Sabbath is a margin. Vacations can be margin throughout the year. Such margins, though, are also needed daily.

I may work long hours, sometimes twelve or more a day, but at the beginning and end of each day I have learned to create time where I'm not doing . . . just being.

This means altering my daily schedule. It has become common for me to go to bed at nine. That's because I get up at five every morning. I enjoy a slow, unrushed morning. I need time to connect to my eternal Father before my day begins. Yes, sleep is important, but this time is just as important.

If I don't schedule margins, I never will have margins, and margins are essential to a healthy life.

Ignoring the Sabbath results in poor health, mind, body, and soul. I have often been reminded by my mentors that if I don't Sabbath, then sickness will become my Sabbath.

Sabbath not only affects physical and mental health, it also reflects spiritual health. God created the rhythm of working six days and resting one. Genesis 2:2 says,

> By the seventh day God completed His work that he had done, and he rested on the seventh day from all His work that he had done. God blessed the seventh day and declared it holy, for on it He rested from His work of creation.

Later He commanded,

> Remember the Sabbath day, to keep it holy: You are to labor six days and do all your work, but the seventh day is a Sabbath to the Lord your god. You must not do any work—you, your son, or daughter, your male or female slave, your livestock, or the foreigner who is within your gates. (EXODUS 20:8–10)

When we work all the time without rest, we are saying to God, "I don't need you, you need me." This attitude reflects a heart of a person that's made an idol of self. This is the attitude of people who have made themselves god.

Health is important, but sometimes healthy practices are counterintuitive. They seem upside down. Often, this is because we don't have a true picture of total health. Physical health receives the greatest emphasis in our society. However, we are more than just physical beings; we are spiritual beings as well. We are eternal.

Sickness has the ability of diminishing one kind of health in order to improve the other.

Consider why so much money is spent on health. Ultimately healthy practices are about extending life. If life is only about what we experience on this planet, then it makes sense to do everything we can to make the most of this life.

However, if there is an eternity, then we must be careful that we don't gain the whole world and lose our soul.

By connecting to eternity, drawing near to God in our sickness, we are reminded that a life to come is always increasing. In that life we'll know no sickness. In that life, there will be complete joy.

CHAPTER

19

SAME SONG, SECOND VERSE

Six months before my diagnosis, Scott, a member of my church in Missouri, received a similar one. Six months after my final surgery, Scott died.

Like my experience, his journey began with a checkup. Scott was feeling tired. He thought there were two possible reasons for his fatigue: his New Year's resolutions to eat healthier and exercise, or his thyroid. Thyroid problems ran in his family.

Scott was employed in the medical field, first as a paramedic, then as a tech in the gastrointestinal lab. Therefore, Scott's doctor respected his concerns. The doctor checked off several boxes on a form to order the necessary tests.

Unintentionally, the doctor ordered a liver panel.

God was in control of the story.

The blood work showed Scott's thyroid was fine, but the liver panel was elevated. With Scott being slightly overweight, the obvious conclusion was fatty-liver disease, but protocol called for an ultrasound. The ultrasound showed some spots on his liver, so it was followed with a CT scan. The CT scan was consistent with metastatic disease, yet no one thought it was cancer. He didn't show any other signs. Nevertheless, a liver biopsy was scheduled.

Three days before his biopsy, Scott was at work when he had alarming symptoms, which led him to immediately schedule a colonoscopy. The next day, after Scott helped the doctor perform colonoscopies on 24 other patients, the same doctor scoped Scott.

Prior to the procedure Scott used a permanent marker to write the phrase *Be gentle* on his rear end.

Scott couldn't control the road ahead, but he was in control of how he walked it.

After the procedure, Scott, his wife, and his father sat with his doctor, who was Scott's friend and boss. With tears in her eyes, she grasped Scott's hands saying, "I'm sorry, my friend. I have to believe that what I saw in your colon is what's in your liver. We've got to get you out of here now."

Scott and his wife rushed to the hospital in St. Louis.

The next several days involved diagnostic tests and consultations with doctors, each getting a chuckle from his marker-tatted rump, a picture of which made it into his charts. Scott would continue to make people laugh. His light-hearted humor was obvious from the words on the shirt he wore to chemotherapy treatments: "Statistics prove five out of five people die."

Cancerous joy had set in.

Treatment included surgery and chemotherapy, none of which were effective in combatting the cancer that had invaded Scott's liver. This became visibly apparent as the cancer squeezed the main bile duct in his liver, making Scott yellow with jaundice.

In the final weeks of his life on earth, while in a car with his children on their way to church, his son asked, "Dad, why isn't there something else they can do?"

Chapter 19

Scott replied, "Now, Tucker, you know they've done everything they can medically. I don't want to leave, but I have to think that it is my time to go, I've done what God has wanted me to do. That's how I have to look at it."

Many people told him, his wife, and his kids, "Your joy, your journey is an inspiration to me."

Cancerous joy is infectious.

Scott's journey gave people a glimpse of the eternal. His story pointed to his Author's story; it glorified his Creator. Scott's story, like mine, wasn't really about Scott. It was about the eternal glory of the One who will be praised forever and ever.

Scott sang of this. With feeble, yellow-tinted hands raised to the sky, he sang praises to God in the weeks before his death. And even when he knew that physical death was certainly near, Scott committed his soul to unending praise to God, from "10,000 Reasons" by Matt Redman, "Ten thousand years and then forevermore."

Scott was walking his path in a way that glorified God.

Scott saw the end. He had faith in Jesus. He didn't wait until his death to do what he is doing now for all eternity: worshipping His Savior, living in peace, eternally satisfied, experiencing complete joy.

STRUGGLE

August 18, 2011

"Dad is in a mood. I still get so frustrated with him. It is hard to ignore. I don't know what to do to make the situation better."

- Because of my self-centered perspective, I had little compassion.

- Because I was focused on finding my own immediate, finite pleasure, I did little to intentionally relieve my father's worry. I never once spoke faithful words to help him see again the eternal truths that had been the foundation of his life.

- Because I wasn't satisfied with my experience, I was unable to help him find eternal satisfaction—upside-down joy.

- Because I didn't know all that was on his mind, I was harsh and judging.

I never dared to consider the struggles I experienced in my relationship with my father were shaping me into the man I would become. I now have a different perspective.

20 PERSPECTIVE

Perspective is the position from which we see something. During my father's life I did not have the perspective I have now. I view him today from a different position.

At least three components influence our perspective: context, time, and relationship.

Context is simply the environment that surrounds us. The urban contexts of Chicago and New York have changed my perspective.

Living and ministering for many years in areas where the absence of dads is noticeable, my perspective of my dad has greatly changed. I now see the importance of having my independence checked and corrected by a godly man throughout my childhood, adolescence, and adulthood. It was important to see a man work day after day to provide for his family. It was important for me to see a man take a stand on controversial issues, even when taking that stand led to backlash and resentment. It was important to have a man in my life that lived with integrity and reverence to his Author and Creator. It was important to see sternness give way to incredible compassion. It was crucial for me to have the earthly love of a father, an incarnate representation of my Heavenly Father's love.

A second factor that influences perspective is time. Time is an interesting thing. Sometimes it passes quickly, other times slowly. There are moments in life where "time flies by," or small moments that seem to last forever. Both phenomena are a glimpse of the true, overarching eternal reality where time is no longer a factor.

The concept of time not being a factor is upside down from the world we know. We live in a world scarce in time. There are several consequences from this mindset.

One consequence is thinking, *I don't have enough time*. We think, *If I only had more time* . . . More time would allow more opportunity to get the things we want. Often we don't know what we want. In ignorance, we fulfill pleasures that are rooted in time, not eternity. We want fulfillment immediately. With this limited perspective, we view the struggles of life as thieves robbing us of pleasure during the limited time we have to enjoy.

What we really want is joy. Joy is timeless, straight from eternity. Nothing—not a person, circumstance or struggle—can rob us of eternal satisfaction.

There's another consequence of a mindset that views time as scarce. We become poor judges of the timeless things God is accomplishing through life's struggles. Much of our world is geared to look for outcomes in a timely manner. If we don't see those outcomes, we think we have failed.

The time I have spent in ministry has helped me develop a better perspective. I realized this eternal mindset when the young man with the broken leg I visited in the hospital ended up in more trouble. A few months after the hospital visit a detective knocked on my door. The detective was looking for my friend so that he could question him regarding a woman that was shot. Apparently ensuing violence and retaliation was the result of my friend's initial injury. A woman on the corner of the street was hit by a stray bullet. The detective believed my friend fired the gun.

There was a lot I didn't know. I didn't know if my friend did it or not. I didn't know what was going to happen to my friend.

But here is what I knew. I knew that God was at work in this young man's life. Based on any timeline, I would have judged my relationship with my friend as a failure. Yet I know that God's timeline is much different. He is authoring the story. He is in control.

Relationships also influence perspective. Knowing someone, taking time to listen to them and find commonalities, will always influence our perspective. It has already been said that perspective yields compassion. My relationship with this young man has yielded compassion for him. He's not a thug in my eyes. Relationships affect how we view others.

When we don't know a person, often our actions are uncompassionate. I experienced this one time with Proof while riding the six o'clock train heading to Manhattan from the Bronx. Typically in subways she slides under the bench, out of sight, out of mind. This day, though, inconspicuous commuting wasn't possible, as the subway was packed with strap-hangers (subway riders, to those not in the know). So I stood holding the pole that extends from the roof to the floor between the rear doors of the car.

At the other end someone caught my eye. He was staring at me. My concern went up when, with eyes fixed on me, he began shuffling past other commuters. Reaching the pole I was grasping, he stuck his middle finger right in my face saying, "I bet you didn't see that, did you?"

It took a moment for me to register and understand the situation. He thought I was blind! The moment was short enough for me to reply, "Actually, I did." With a jolt he rushed away, bobbing back and forth around the other subway riders. I doubt if he knew me he would have acted with so little compassion.

The power of relationships to influence perspective became clear to me one summer when a mission team from down south was helping our ministry host a sports camp in a neighborhood park. During the camp, some unattended backpacks were stolen. The next day as I chatted with some teens that were part of our summer program, I noticed they turned their attention from me to four guys walking across the baseball field.

They were big guys. One had arms the size of barrels. Another stood over six feet tall, with muscles that pressed the veins against his skin. The other two may have been smaller, but they had a crazy look in their eyes. The company that surrounded me was visibly uncomfortable as they shifted their weight from one foot to another.

I wasn't scared.

Why?

Not because I was big enough or skilled enough to go "Chuck Norris" on them. I wasn't scared because I knew them. They were my friends.

The ringleader asked with a thick Puerto Rican accent and broken English, "Andrew, you OK?"

"Yeah. I'm great."

"Somebody rob you?"

"Uh, no. That was yesterday and it wasn't me. It was some people that left their backpacks hanging on the fence."

"Oh, OK. Let us know if you need us."

My friends came ready to knock some heads. As they walked away, one of the teens next to me said, "Andrew, you've got goons!"

I replied, "Yeah, I do, and you better never forget it."

From the teens' perspectives, these men were a threat because they didn't know them. They had no relationship. But I knew them. Because of my perspective, because of my relationship, I saw these men very differently.

Context, time, and relationships all influence our perspective. They help to change the way we think.

All three have changed the way I see my dad. As I age, I realize I am becoming more like my dad. I'm starting to look like him. My bald head is just one proof. Our family used to poke fun at my dad for going to bed and getting up early, preferring baths over showers, and walking around our house in his red-and-black plaid pajamas. These pajamas always reminded me of a checkerboard. Two of my greatest simple pleasures now are taking a long bath and wearing my comfortable white bathrobe around my apartment.

Context, time, and relationships not only changed my thinking but also changed me.

CHAPTER

21 AN ETERNAL PERSPECTIVE

Context, time, and relationships are part of the natural workings of the world around us. It doesn't take an eternal mindset for these to affect our perspective. There are, however, at least two components that influence our perspective that are straight from eternity: wisdom and revelation. Both are the outcome of having an eternal mindset.

The person who wrote Psalm 97 certainly had an eternal mindset. Read what he wrote:

> The Lord reigns! Let the earth rejoice; let the many coasts and islands be glad. Clouds and thick darkness surround Him; righteousness and judgment are the foundation of His throne. Fire goes before Him and burns up His foes on every side. His lightning lights up the world; the earth sees and trembles. The mountains melt like wax at the presence of the Lord—at the presence of the Lord of all the earth. The heavens proclaim His righteousness; all the peoples see his glory. All who serve carved images, those who boast in idols, will be put to shame. All the gods must worship Him. (vv. 97:1–7)

From his writing, we can see what he sees. He has a vision of God. He has a theophany. A theophany is a little like an epiphany. An epiphany is a moment of clear thought where all things come together and suddenly make sense. A light bulb is turned on. A theophany is God turning on the light bulb.

What does the psalmist see? He clearly sees that God reigns!

This is both an already-and-not-yet reality. It is both a vision of things as they really are, and also what they will be.

In this vision of the end, there are two responses. Some rejoice and others are ashamed. In God's kingdom, where He reigns with all knowledge, all power, and all rightful authority, what would cause some to be ashamed?

It's not a mystery in this passage. It clearly says, "All who serve carved images, those who boast in idols, will be put to shame" (97:7).

They are ashamed because they valued something above God. They were attracted to something besides God. They were devoted to something besides God. They worshipped something besides God.

Those who worship anything or anyone besides God will be ashamed.

We don't have to look far to see what people worship. The social media site Facebook is little more than a shrine to self. The majority of entries on my newsfeed are pictures of food, vacations, politics, crude humor, sexual innuendo, and even pornographic images. Each entry is an offering laid before the idol of the god of self. Facebook is the modern equivalent of the golden calf, except we are the calves.

Of course, the world around us doesn't always display things as they really are. The psalmist saw the eternal truth.

He saw God with claps of lightning, rolls of thunder, melting mountains like wax! God is all-powerful.

The psalmist saw a world rejoicing because of God's judgments; these judgments were good because God is all-knowing.

Even in this theophany, clouds and darkness surround God. Darkness cloaks our ability to see things as they really are. When I was a child, my siblings took great pleasure in turning the lights off while I was in the basement. My mind would see contorted images of monsters in the dark of the basement. Flipping on the light showed my fears were baseless.

There were things the psalmist could not see clearly, perhaps because sometimes the circumstances of life prevent us from seeing the truth. We don't see things as they really are.

My dad had difficulty seeing. His eyesight was fine, but he didn't always see himself accurately. I realized this a few days after writing the journal entry at the beginning of this section. Driving from our farm to town in his gray SUV, we talked in a manner that was rare for us.

With eyes on the road as my dad navigated the curves and hills not far from our little farm he reflected, "I haven't contributed anything to the world that you kids can be proud of."

His struggles loomed so large that he couldn't see his greatest contribution: his kids. My brother is a teacher, my sister a school counselor, and I'm a missionary. Each one of us found ways to better the world.

My dad needed a different perspective. I know I often need a different perspective. I need an eternal perspective. I need wisdom and revelation.

Wisdom is the ability to see things as they really are; revelation is seeing eternal truth. Both are granted by God. God gives us eyes to see things as they really are and to see eternal truth, but we have to look for it.

Too often we look at our struggle rather than God. Struggles can dominate our landscape. They often look bigger than they are. I can hold my thumb up to the night sky and blot out the moon. I wouldn't be very wise if I thought my finger was bigger than the moon.

Similarly, when we focus on the struggles right before us, they loom very large. The eternal truth is different. Looking at our struggles in the context of time, not eternity, prevents us from seeing the eternal truth, to see what God is doing, to see the story He is writing.

Wisdom and revelation not only help us see eternity better, they help us understand life on this side of eternity. My perspective of my struggles with my dad was skewed. I was unable to see how those struggles were shaping me in the long run.

I wanted picturesque, fatherly moments with my dad like I saw while sitting on the yellow beanbag in our basement watching *Full House*. Father and child had struggles, but Danny always resolved the problem with sage words, a hug, and a kiss.

That's the story I would have written. From my perspective in those days, that story would have made me feel better. But I wonder, *how would I be different today?*

Now my perspective is different. It's changed because of context, time, and relationships. God has given me wisdom to see things as they really are. I now know more of the eternal truth because God has revealed it to me.

My greatest struggle years ago used to give me frustration. Today it gives me joy. That's just a little upside down.

22 JOSHUA'S STORY

Listening and learning from others has helped me gain perspective for the struggles of my life. We don't have to look far to find someone who has greater struggles than the ones we face. These people can teach us a lot.

Among the many people that have helped me is a friend from my hometown. Initially a friend of my grandma, then a friend of my parents, he became closer to me when he generously gave me a trip to New York as a senior gift in high school. I experienced the city for the first time with him.

I spent some time talking with him recently about his experience with struggle. We met in a park one warm, summer day. Sitting across the wooden picnic table from me was a man I had grown to respect. With a gentle breeze blowing, sitting next to a small pond alive with fish swirls and frogs hopping, we were meeting to talk about his grandson whom I will call Joshua.

Born to his teen daughter, this eight-pound, twelve-ounce grandson with the stocky shoulders of a linebacker got stuck in the birth canal. This caused Joshua to stroke. The stroke caused a lack of air and a lack of blood to his brain.

The little boy spent the first five weeks of his life in a children's hospital. Beyond just treatment, doctors looked for the cause. Joshua's mom felt like she was on trial as the doctors asked, "Do you have seizures? Did you take drugs? Did you smoke?"

My friend was sitting next to his daughter during the inquiries. He recalled, "You sit there like you're guilty, like you're before a jury."

She hadn't done any of those things.

The hospital would become a familiar place for this family as Joshua underwent multiple procedures there. To prevent reflux, doctors put in a button and wrapped off his stomach. For the rest of his life, he would be fed through a feeding tube. For the first two years, despite this procedure, he continued to vomit. The fluid would aspirate into his lungs. He had pneumonia 50 times before he was three. Brittle bones from lack of use broke five times, none of which he even felt.

As I listened to my friend describe his grandson's injuries, they sounded horrifying to me. But my friend helped me understand better, saying, "He doesn't really have pain sensations. He's had a broken leg five times and didn't even know it was broken. He never cried. His brain center is not like yours or mine."

There was, however, one time that Joshua felt pain. His leg was cast because of another broken bone, but it wasn't the broken bone that hurt.

My friend explained, "When they put a cast on him, you can't tell what's going on under the cast. So if something bad is happening under the cast, you don't know it."

"One day he was really hollering, kicking, and flinging his arms and legs. We couldn't figure out what was happening. We unwrapped the plastic to see what was going on. At the bottom of his heel, the tissue had rotted, about the size of a quarter, all the way down to his bone. His skin was black. Black as black can be. I guess he had finally had enough. He was ticked off. He knew what that pain was."

Despite all of the many health issues and complications, Joshua survived. With constant, 24-hours-a-day care, Joshua grew into a boy, then a teenager. Day after day, Joshua was fed every 15 minutes through a feeding tube, his mouth was swabbed out with a toothette, and his underwear was changed after he used the bathroom.

A person might attribute Joshua's survival to the many procedures or the expertise of doctors. To me, his survival is tied to one person. Most of Joshua's life had been spent in the arms of the man I sat across from on that sunny day, arms that held him while they gently rocked back and forth in a rocking chair.

Such compassionate care had an unforeseen, inevitable, yet unpreventable consequence. Joshua's spine curved. Like a tree adapting to its environment, his body grew nearly the opposite direction from many years of being held in the same position.

My friend stated matter-of-factly, "Eventually they say that will be his Doomsday. His lungs will be crushed. He won't be able to breathe."

Reflecting, he continued, "You don't see him as a child lying there who cannot communicate, who cannot feed, who cannot sit up, who can't do one thing for himself. Even the lowest animal . . ."

Tears came to his eyes as he paused to catch his breath.

"When I am out here running or walking in this park, I look at the path and see earthworms crossing. A lot of them don't make it, especially in sunshine when the black top is hot.

"I tell myself, *That earthworm is probably just about as intelligent as my grandson.* My grandson has no . . ."

His words became a whisper and disappeared. "I don't know if I can really do this or not. This is pretty tough stuff."

He picked up the napkin from lunch and wiped his face.

"When I go by them I think, *They aren't going to make it. They can't live in this 90-degree temperature and get across this black asphalt.* So I stop and look to see if they're crawling or moving any more. I pick them up and throw them in the grass. I tell myself, *Self, why do you even care about that earthworm? This is really about as low of life of animal that you can probably have.*

"But still I feel like I have to give them a chance. They might be going to a party some place. I always stop, throw them to the side, and allow them to start over.

"Joshua is basically like that. He can't do anything. Really, I think an earthworm can do more than he can. He is unique in the sense that he doesn't feed or move his hands, feet, arms, or legs. He doesn't do anything on his own."

My friend's tone changed slightly as he said, "He's not supposed to be able to hear, not supposed to be able to see. But sometimes he can look up at you, and you just know he's seeing you. I come down in the morning from my bedroom, he'll be sleeping, and as soon as he hears me coming down the stairs, he wakes up. So he's got to hear something. It's not that he can't hear; it's just he can't . . ."

Trying to help me understand, he explained, "If a person is blind, they can't see out of their eyes. It's not that my grandson can't see out of his eyes; it's that he can't relay the message from his eyes to his brain, because there's really no brain there to relay it to. Same thing with hearing, I guess, it's not that he can't hear the noise; his brain can't tell him what that noise is."

His voice lifted a little as he said, "But you tell yourself he does hear you and he does see you, and he does enjoy it. He is just as human as you or me. He has emotions like us too. He wants to be known. He wants to be loved. He wants to be hugged. He wants to be kissed. He wants to be acknowledged. He wants to be a part of us and a part of our little house."

My friend paused a moment.

It was clear many thoughts had been filed in the cabinet of his mind. As we talked he would take one out, show it to me, and put it back in. Then he would take another out and allow me to learn a little more about his perspective, about his struggle.

Occasionally it seemed as if the conversation was about to end. But it would continue. It was almost as if he was collecting the files from his mind which he had lay on the table before me. Putting them away to leave, he would find another thought which until that day nobody had seen but him.

He continued talking as if he saw the file labeled, "Earthworm." "For that reason, you think you need to do all you can do to try to keep him happy. Because that's what you're really supposed to do. Like the earthworm, you're not supposed to step on them and walk over them."

CHAPTER

23   24 HOURS WITH JOSHUA

My friend has learned a lot from his own struggles, as well as the struggles of Joshua. As we sat beneath a sprawling oak tree, he told me, "There's so much you can really say about a child like that and your experience with a child like that. This experience has allowed me to understand a few things about this ol' life."

Struggles have given him new perspectives.

First, he's found a sense of purpose and meaning in his life that is transcendent. It goes beyond the temporary pleasures he could secure for himself as a successful businessman.

He told me, "People ask, 'Why are you taking care of your grandson like that?'"

"Because I love it. It's exhausting, especially at night; but on the other side of the story I do love it. I love that I'm doing something for somebody, doing something to make this child happy. When I am there with him at nighttime, I wouldn't care if the world stopped turning. I'm perfectly happy right there. I have enough money. I could live anywhere I want to live, go anywhere I want to go, do anything that I want to do. The one thing out of all that I want to do is be there with him."

Second, his struggles have led him to questions, primarily questions on what is of true worth in this life.

He shared with me a fantasy from his mind. "I've always said a million times, I would give anything for him to be able to eat a hamburger and drink a Coca-Cola. You know, people don't appreciate anything really. My grandson has never had anything in his mouth before, any food or substance."

"You always think, *If I could just have my grandson normal for one day . . . Just one day. Just 24 hours. What would we do in those 24 hours? What kind of joy would we share?*

"I wouldn't want him just to have joy though. I would want him to experience some sadness. I would want him to experience exhilaration in a thousand different ways, experience being in love with a female, experience touching a female, experience all kinds of different joys, excitements, ups and downs. I've always thought that would be a great book to write: *24 Hours with Joshua.*

"If I could do 24 different things for 24 hours, one hour at a time, what would I do? What would he do? What would we do? What would we see? What would we eat? What kind of feelings would we have?

"What would be the 24 things that would most teach him about our entire life? It wouldn't only be good feelings. What are the 24 most important things to you as a human being?

"How much trouble could he make? That's part of life too, isn't it? Isn't part of life doing some things that don't hurt anyone, just a little ornery. Drink a beer, do a little gambling, maybe do something that's 'common, but not common.'

"I always thought it would be wonderful to have just 24 hours. I would trade everything in the world for that, if he could have one day."

As I listened to my friend, I was amused by how his perspective and my perspective often differed. We were indeed an unlikely pair. His Catholic upbringing, colorful language, and enjoyment of a beer or two are stark contrasts to this teetotaler Baptist missionary.

Our faith has always been a difference that is apparent to me and seemingly always a question in my friend's mind. A few moments before we started talking about his grandson, my friend and I had talked about eternity.

Chapter 23

My friend told me a story. "One time when I was a senior in high school, my teacher wanted me to write an essay about something. I wrote it about dying. When I got to heaven, there was all the wonderful gold and glitter in the world. There were houses, cars, food, luxury, and excitement, everything that has ever put a smile on your face. Anything you could want in this entire world was there: love with other people, caring, everything in the world was there.

"Everything you wanted was right in front of you, but nobody ever smiled. I told myself, *Golly, I don't see anyone smiling.*

"Then one day I was walking down the street and saw a license plate. Below the numbers was written *hell*.

"I wasn't in heaven at all. I was in hell.

"People weren't smiling because they couldn't escape the thought, *If this is hell, what's heaven like?*

"They were thinking, *I missed something, didn't I?*

"For the rest of their life, they told themselves, *If this is hell, how can I smile knowing there's something else up there even greater than this? I'll never be happy, because I'll never be there. I'll never experience that.*"

Hearing my friend's story caused me to reflect. To live life without the hope of eternity is bleak. Without an eternal perspective, there is no meaning to any of the struggles we encounter. My perspective is to view all struggles from the perspective of eternity. My friend doesn't share my view.

Yet I sat listening in wonder at the eternal truths that emerged from his lips.

"Far, far away the most important thing, nothing is even in the dust, is to love somebody, knowing that they love you because you love them. Without my grandson I never would have known what love is all about. He taught me what it is. He taught me that love doesn't come with gold, diamonds, earrings, glory, music, and all the other stuff that's supposed to make you happy in this world.

"Love is all you need to experience in this life. You don't have to experience all this other stuff. If you've got love, you don't need anything else."

Looking straight at me with concern in his eyes he said, "I'm sure that in your church, with your God and all . . . I hope you have that same feeling, I hope you honestly do. You think that being with God and being just you and him . . ."

I interrupted and said, "Honestly, I feel like I'm your grandson in the hands of a loving Father."

CHAPTER

24 THREAD

The struggles of his life have given my friend a perspective to see deeper truths. These truths, viewed in the context of my faith, show the Author of our story revealing Himself and the true eternal reality.

My friend's story is a vivid picture of our Author's love for us. We are like worms. We are nothing more than Joshua compared to our Creator. Our life is sustained by His care.

Sometimes we live unaware of this truth; other times it is apparent. Yet, we will never fully understand the extent of the Father's sacrifice. We will never fully comprehend the depths of His love for us. But that doesn't mean though we shouldn't try!

The Apostle Paul prayed that we would be granted wisdom and revelation to see the depths of God's love. Here is what he said, "I pray that you, being rooted and firmly established in love, may be able to comprehend with all the saints what is the length and width, height and depths of god's love, and to know the Messiah's love that surpasses knowledge, so that you may be filled with all the fullness of God" (Ephesians 3:17–19).

John was one that knew God's love. He was described as the "one Jesus loved" (John 13:23). He knew love came straight from God. He said, "We love because he first loved us" (1 John 4:19).

We can know God and we can love Him because He loved us first. However, He doesn't need us; we need him. My friend has a hard time understanding this truth. He has found true love from his grandson. This love though was a love that my friend needed.

He described it as he talked about Joshua saying, "You love him and he loves you. Nothing is attached to that. You have no reason to love him other than the fact that he exists. No other reason. He is part of me. This child needed somebody to love him. That's where I come in. On the other side of the story, I honestly needed someone to love me too.

"Here's a child that doesn't have an EKG showing anything is even happening in his brain. You think to yourself, *Who cares?! This person loves me. I love him.* You don't have to say it."

With hopelessness in his voice my friend continued, "I would like for him to say it one day though."

We all have a longing inside us to love and be loved. A lot of us have never experienced true love; we have settled for counterfeit love.

My friend has seen this in the everyday lives of people around him.

He told me, "A lot of people get married and have children. They go through life and say, 'I love you.'"

His tone rose as he continued, "Do you really? Do you really think you love them, or are you just saying it? I think about couples saying, 'I was in love, but I don't love you anymore; I fell out of love; I'm getting a divorce; you've changed and I've changed.'

"Come on guys. Did you really love 'em to begin with?

"If you really love them, you are going to give everything you've got in this lifetime—every physical and mental part of your life. Not an hour goes by that I don't think about Joshua."

My friend's comments have helped me reflect on the nature of true love. True love is eternal; it transcends inconvenience.

This quality of love was clearly present in my friend's relationship with Joshua when he plainly stated, "If Joshua were to go to the bathroom 65 times an hour, and I had to change him 65 times an hour, and I had to hold him in my lap from now until the day he dies, for every minute of the rest of his life, that's what I would do. I would do it because I love him. No matter if he just did his drawers, two seconds later did them again, and two seconds later did them again. There's nothing he could possibly do to me to stop me from loving him."

Thinking about my friend's experience has caused me to realize love is a thread from eternity. When it is ripped apart from eternity, it becomes like everything else: scarce, temporary, and reciprocal.

The eternal truth is God offers abundant, eternal love. He doesn't need our love. He is entirely sufficient. His love for us is so complete, so abundant, that He entered into our existence and became like us.

Jesus is the embodiment of our Father's love. As His Son, before we ever knew Him, before we ever loved Him, Jesus traded places with us.

Consider Jesus' words when he said, "No one has greater love than this, that someone would lay down his life for his friends" (John 15:13). He said no greater love exists than giving one's life for another.

He not only taught this truth; He lived it! In love, He gave His life for me.

Because of His sacrificial love, my faith in Jesus as Author and Creator grants me life and extends my life. Each new moment is part of a forever-expanding life. I am not dying, but living forever. I therefore have unlimited time, unlimited resources, unlimited love. I am eternally satisfied. I have joy.

Only in Jesus does a person find such fullness of joy. Other experiences may give us a small taste, but they don't fill us up.

So often we think of our lives like a reservoir, a place to collect love like water. The problem with collected water is stagnation. Stagnant water brings sickness, decay, and death. Instead, Jesus described joy like the Jacks Fork River my dad and I would ride along on our horses. It moves. It flows (John 7:38).

Yes, we do have a reservoir in our soul that needs to be filled with love, but it must come from outside of us. It must come from the One who can give it without losing it.

But it can't only flow in; it must also flow out. It flows to others but also back to the One who gave it to us. Not because He needs it, but because we are fulfilled by loving Him. We are made complete. We are eternally satisfied. We have joy.

My friend doesn't have this perspective yet. However, my friend isn't faithless. Much of his faith has been placed in science, reason, and intellect.

Through science he has marveled at the existence of life. During embryology class in college he studied reproduction.

He fondly recalled, "Two cells become four. Four cells become eight, 16, 32, 64, 128, 256. Then there is 'The Ball.' It's a ball of cells, a round mass of cells that at a seemingly random moment in time starts descending. Together they become the GI tract. Then more cells descend becoming the heart. At some point the heart starts beating."

With a glimmer in his eye he mused, "It's an absolute marvel!"

My friend sees this marvel and uses science to understand the randomness. I see the same marvel and stand in awe of a divine Author who is in control of the randomness.

We view the same information from two different perspectives. My friend's perspective affects how he views the world, and so does mine. Science has a perspective of the universe that is ever-expanding and never-ending, yet we are forever-dying. We are bound by death, giving us limited time, limited resources, and limited love.

My perspective is upside down from this. I am forever-increasing in life, no longer bound by death, unlimited in time, abundant in my Father's resources, blessed by His gracious love.

However, my friend's experience with struggle has given him new lenses to see the world. Science doesn't explain everything for him. Science doesn't explain the deep truths he has learned from his grandson.

Struggle may be my friend's salvation. His grandson has helped him see eternal truths that never made sense before.

Here is a truth that might seem upside down to some. Joshua isn't a struggle. He's a blessing.

I know that's how my friend sees it. I pray that he will grab that thread and trace it back to the fabric of eternity.

25 REJOICE. BE PATIENT. PRAY.

Struggle is a backdrop for the human experience. God's Word says that struggle is unavoidable. Numerous are the stories of men and women who encounter troubling circumstances: Adam, Eve, Cain, Abel, Abraham, Isaac, Jacob, Joseph, Moses, David, Elijah, Elisha, Ruth, Esther, Job, Mary, Joseph, Jesus, Peter. . . . Do I need to keep going?

Some of these individuals from the Bible set an example of glorifying God through struggle. Some did not. Almost all did a little of both. In each of these stories, it wasn't their circumstances that determined the outcome. It was their response.

Paul was one figure that responded in ways that glorified God. He viewed his entire life in the shadow of eternity. He faced significant struggle. He went from being the persecutor to the persecuted. He was beaten, thrown in jail, hated by the Jews, and not understood by some of the Christians.

Paul explained in his letter to the Romans that we glorify God in struggle not by minimizing and avoiding affliction, but by maximizing it. He said, "We also rejoice in our afflictions, because we know that affliction produces endurance, endurance produces proven character, and proven character produces hope" (Romans 5:3–4).

In short, affliction leads to endurance, which builds character, which gives hope. Hope is continually looking forward to heaven.

Here is a simple truth that has changed my thinking: *I don't want to be in heaven what I am now.* God agrees.

At the beginning of this book, I talked about the fish in the farm pond at my mom's house. They live unaware of the surrounding world, a world that is eternal compared to theirs. Here's the thing, though. Even if they wanted to live in our world, they couldn't, because they don't have the ability to breathe outside of their world.

In our earthly, human state, we have no ability to breathe the air of heaven. God first has to make us a new creation but then has to teach us how to breathe. He has to make us like Him.

Paul is telling the church in Rome that God makes us like Him through tribulation.

Paul also knew his response to struggles could impact others' eternity.

Some say that we can be so heavenly minded that we are no earthly good. The reverse is really the problem. We are so earthly minded that we are no heavenly good.

Several years ago while at Bear Mountain State Park in upstate New York, I saw something that was thought-provoking. Inside the park is a zoo of animals common to the area. In one of the cages were several vultures. They had food but were locked down. On the outside of this cage were many more vultures. They wanted in. All they could focus on was the food. They didn't see the cage. They also didn't see the unlimited potential that existed in their surrounding world.

The ones that were free not only didn't live in freedom; they also had no ability to proclaim that freedom to their comrades in prison.

How fixated we too become on others' earthly blessings, failing to think about our eternal blessing. Struggles provide our most profound opportunities to point others toward eternity. We can only do this if we have an eternal mindset.

Mindset is so important. It is amazing how powerful the mind is.

I learned this during my chemotherapy treatments. In anticipation of them, I would sometimes start thinking about the treatment process. If I thought in detail about the IVs, the Etoposide and Cisplatin, the many times a phlebotomist would unsuccessfully search for my "chemo-veins" only to try once again, I would get sick. I would actually feel nauseous.

Paul knew that mindset was important. He described his mindset when he said, "Rejoice in hope; be patient in affliction; be persistent in prayer" (Romans 12:12).

We should rejoice even when we don't feel like rejoicing. Not only does it bring glory to God, but it also changes our mindset. It changes our mood.

And yet, it does no good to lie. There is no benefit to God or us to offer an insincere praise. We must find reason to rejoice.

People with an eternal mindset sincerely rejoice because they are focused on the end. They know that all struggles are temporary. One day they will be relieved from all tribulation. They have hope. They know that all circumstances are working together for their final good.

Living with the end in mind, the eternally minded person is able to be patient in affliction. He or she is empowered knowing God can bring a whole lot of good out of a whole lot of bad.

Sometimes it feels like the greatest afflictions in our life are people. Through my years of ministering in Chicago and the Bronx, I have learned that relationships with people can be rocky at times. I have had important people, people I care about, people I love respond in ways that hurt. But I didn't have to move to the city to encounter relationship struggles; I had already experienced relational turmoil with my dad.

I think Paul is telling us to be patient with people who afflict us. Why? Because we have hope. Hope that God is working to bring good for their lives.

What do we do for those people?

We do the same thing for these people that we should be doing for ourselves, persisting in prayer. We can either be constant in prayer—persisting, persevering, and habitually praying—or we can be inconstant—praying randomly, sporadically, or not at all.

A person living upside down approaches struggles differently. They persist in prayer; they are patient in affliction; they always rejoice. The upside down life is upside down because they are rooted in God's eternal love by having a relationship with Jesus. For them, tribulation doesn't destroy joy; it refines it.

The most valuable precious metals are the ones that are the most free from other contaminants. Life is filled with many worthless impurities. They are worthless because they aren't eternal.

Our relationship with Jesus imparts an entirely different mindset. Looking back, He overcame death, the only struggle that is common to all of humanity. Looking ahead, He's coming back to permanently put an end to all struggle.

If Jesus returns tomorrow, why should I feel defeated today?

Paul had this mindset. It was clear when he said,

> *What does it matter? Just that in every way, whether out of false motives or true, Christ is proclaimed. And in this I rejoice. . . . My eager expectation and hope is that I will not be ashamed about anything, but that now as always with boldness, Christ will be highly honored in my body, whether by life or by death. For me, living is Christ and dying is gain. . . . Live your life in a manner that is worthy of the Gospel of Christ.* (PHILIPPIANS 1:18–20, 27)

I too can have this mindset. I can rejoice always, be patient in affliction, and persistent in prayer because no matter what struggle I face—whether I live or die—I am always on the cusp of eternity.

DEATH

December 19, 2011
"Andrew, something happened.... Your dad passed away."

Following the funeral, a caravan of cars drove 30 miles to a veterans' cemetery where his ashes were buried. For many the cracks of gunshots fired by a firing squad at a military funeral reverberate in the heart with echoes of hopelessness. As I listened and the folded red, white, and blue flag was handed to my mom, there were a lot of things that seemed uncertain.

There was a lot I didn't understand. However, through his death I began to understand the certainty of hope that sprouts from the root of faith.

CHAPTER

26

CREMATING THE PIG

In Harper Lee's *To Kill a Mockingbird*, Atticus tells Scout, "You never really understand a person until you consider things from his point of view . . . until you climb into his skin and walk around in it."

For the two weeks that followed my dad's funeral, I developed a whole new understanding of my father. We have already said that perspective yields compassion. Perspective also gives understanding.

In those first few weeks after my dad's death, I was able to see from his perspective. I lived his life. I literally walked in his shoes when I wore his rubber boots to do his chores around the farm. I got up in the morning and walked across the frozen ground toward the red barn. The grass crunched under my feet as I breathed in the cold morning air. The horses said, "Hello," with their whinnies, knowing they were about to be fed. They watched peculiarly as I cleaned out the stalls. It almost seemed as if they knew something had changed.

I also tried to get a grip on all of the loose strings from his business and personal life that needed to be tied up. I began to understand my father better than I had my entire life. My perspective was different than a few months before, when I was so frustrated with him.

I was now largely responsible for my dad's kingdom. That kingdom had a name—M Pines. This wasn't the place of my birth or my childhood. When I was in college, my parents had moved to this 45-acre farm named after the many pine trees that lined the property. It was an idyllic environment for my dad to enjoy his family and vice versa for the last ten years of his life. We all have fond memories of bonfires by the cabin, riding horses in the arena, and fishing in the pond.

Twice I was able to bring kids from Chicago and New York to visit. On one of these occasions, we decided to roast a whole pig in the ground. The plan was to treat the boys from the city to an old-fashioned potluck. We invited about a hundred folks and even had a bluegrass band.

The night before the event, the boys got to see the whole hog before we buried it. To them bacon came from the store. Their eyes were opened wide that night.

We buried the pig.

Through the night I knew something wasn't right. From my bed in the cabin where all the boys and leaders were staying, I saw flames coming up from the ground. Half a dozen times I took a shovel and covered the flames with dirt.

The next morning the hole was uncovered, and a tractor pulled up the metal sheet that was used to lower the hog into the hole. My dad removed the hot metal that covered the pig before burial. We stood puzzled. There was no pig!

We looked down in the cavernous space below. The pig wasn't there either.

Best we could tell, we had cremated the pig!

These memories and many others paraded through my mind in the weeks after my dad's death. His worries marched through as well. I felt the weight of securing all my dad had worked so hard to provide.

My father was a hard worker. He worked at his business and his farm chores literally until the day he died. One of my tasks in the weeks following his death was to destroy his confidential real-estate appraisal work. This tedious work had consumed so much of his time for so many years.

In the city they use gigantic shredders the size of trailers. In small-town Missouri, we burn it!

As I tended the fire with a rake, gradually adding more papers to it, the dancing flames drew me into deeper thought. Nearly 20 years of my dad's work went up in smoke in about three hours. All that was left were ashes.

I began to contemplate where I spend my time. I, like my dad, tend to work very hard.

As I added more papers to the fire, I began to ask myself, *What is truly valuable?*

Things of value endure. They last. In New York City one can find cheap purses and watches in Chinatown. Although they may look like their more expensive counterparts, they are more cheaply made and thus fall apart. Their more expensive twins, in comparison, last much longer. They often even come with a lifetime guarantee.

Earthly blessings are always decreasing in value. Consider modern technology. A few years ago I purchased a popular cell phone. The purchase price after discounts was $200. Years later, the same phone might be bought for 99 cents.

The blessings we seek tend to be of the earthly sort, their value always decreasing. So we often go to God in prayer, asking for blessings. Our prayers often become a checklist for the increase of our kingdom. These prayers are not necessarily selfish in nature. We ask for the benefit of our families, our ministries, or others we love.

M Pines was not a place for my dad's glory to be on display. It was a place for his family. The same is true for his work. His work paid for me to go to college. It provided a place for my niece to ride horses behind my dad, grasping his belt loops as I once did. It was not only a place for him, but also for others, to enjoy.

Nevertheless, I stared at the fire and understood: *Just like the pig, so too are our kingdoms.* Not just our kingdoms but our bodies as well. My dad was cremated. All that remained of him and his work were ashes.

God wants to free us from the bondage of a life that is forever decreasing in value. Jesus taught this when he said, "Don't collect for yourselves treasures on earth, where moth and rust destroy and where thieves break in and steal. But collect for yourselves treasures in heaven, where neither moth nor rust destroys, and where thieves don't break in and steal" (Matthew 6:19–20).

Later in the same chapter, He said, "Seek first the kingdom of God and His righteousness, and all these things will be provided for you" (v. 33). In others words, we should seek God's eternal kingdom rather than building our own kingdoms because, in the end, our kingdoms have no value.

As I watched the smoke rise from the bonfire that consumed my dad's paperwork, I processed several scenarios and potential problems for the weeks and months ahead. I wanted to provide security for my family.

I asked myself, *What's possible?*

In my kingdom, so much of what I faced seemed impossible. Our kingdoms exist only within the realm of the possible. We can only do what we can do. It's common to be so surrounded by problems we have no power to resolve, much less find joy in.

Then it hit me!

I remembered the words of a devotion from Eugene Petersen's *God's Message for Each Day*, which I had read that morning: "[God] is free above and beyond what we observe of his ways. He is free to do whatever he wills, whether it conforms to what we have observed as the laws He established in creation or not."

In God's kingdom, anything is possible!

I knew this in other areas of my life. Most people would take one look at me and think, *There's no way he lives in the Bronx, much less pastors a church in the Bronx.* I am short, fair-skinned with freckles, younger, bald, and small-town. I am not likely the person someone would pick to do the job I'm doing.

I've always loved the irrationality of my calling.

God's plan seems irrational to us sometimes. But His plan doesn't have to make sense to us. He may seem irrational, but only because we don't know all that He knows.

I have always identified with Abraham's story. It wasn't rational for Abraham to leave his home. It didn't make much sense that he would father a nation when his wife was barren. His wife Sarah laughed at the thought because she didn't understand.

How silly her disbelief must have looked to God. God asked Abraham, "Why did Sarah laugh, saying, 'Can I really have a baby when I'm old?' Is anything impossible for the LORD?" (Genesis 18:13–14).

Later, Abraham raised a knife, ready to kill the very son God had miraculously provided (ch. 22). How insane!

None of Abraham's story makes sense—at least not from Abraham's perspective.

Faith doesn't require things to make sense. In fact, true faith trusts and obeys when it doesn't make sense, when we don't understand.

I've learned, over the years, if we want to run toward God, then we must run toward the impossible. With man things are impossible. Not with God—all things are possible through Him. (See Matthew 19:26.)

I began to look at life differently that morning. I had a new understanding of what was truly valuable. I also had a new way of looking at the problems before me. I stopped asking, "What can I do to fix the problems?" and instead asked, "What can God do?"

27 RAINBOW BRIDGE, RATTLESNAKES, AND HOPE

When a person dies, there are many different responses. Living in a neighborhood where unexpected death is commonplace, people here are quick to share sentimentalities such as, "God needed another angel. . . . He is in a better place. . . . Her soul is finally at rest."

Then there is the superstition and mysticism. The older Catholic women—*viejas*, as they are called in our neighborhood—will gather, lighting candles and chanting for a week following a person's death. They hope their actions will improve their loved one's eternal outcome.

Certainly our response to death reveals what we believe about God and eternity. Our responses reveal how little we understand.

Do we believe that we somehow work our way into a better existence? Have we even spent much time thinking about death?

It's been said the only two things certain in this world are death and taxes. I wonder sometimes, *Why are so many people uncertain about the only certain thing?*

As I sat with my dog in the chair outside baggage claim the morning of my dad's death, I spent some time thinking about him. He was a person who had thought about death. Through my adolescence and early adulthood, many of our beloved family pets had passed away. He wrote an obituary for each one.

Here is one obituary he wrote when a horse named Stemwinder died:

Hello kids,

Well Stemwinder has crossed the rainbow bridge into our memories. She was buried this day under the pine trees out in front of our home with her son, RB, and good friend, Bobby Sue, and Curly Sue, and Belle watching. [Each of those was a family pet.]

I am sure that her last three or four days were not real pleasant as you know she never liked to be inside. I had brought her in the barn before I went after a trailer as I could tell she was not feeling well. Your Mom called Webb to come check on her on Monday night and he gave her a shot to ease some pain she had. I checked on her when I got in last night, and could tell she was not doing well. She gave me a look that to me said I am not going to be around long. I intended to take her to the vet this morning, but found her this morning in the stall. I knew when I looked in the stall what the situation was.

What I will remember about Stemwinder is you kids. You grew up around her. She was five when she came into our family, and come April 8, she would have been 27. We watched her with her two colts, and when I think of her I will think about us riding at Eminence, and the family times we had with our horses. I could say a lot more, but I am having trouble seeing through my tears. I used to be embarrassed to cry, but I am not any more. Time does that to you.

This has been a hard day for me, but I am glad that we had Stemwinder, and memories will come back. You each will probably have some small memory that will come back either about a ride or an experience that was had with Stemwinder in the picture. No matter where we go now we will always remember that M Pines is where Stemwinder is buried.

Love, Dad Mann
January 17, 2007

When Barney our barn cat and my sister's Pomeranian, named Rocky, died, he wrote about them crossing that same rainbow bridge.

Despite all the struggles I had with my dad and all the struggles that would be ahead from his unexpected death, I knew he had prepared for his death.

He had faith, a commitment to his eternal Father. That faith was not based on the works of his life but instead on the work of Jesus, God's Son. As a result of such faith, God promises eternity forever with Him.

My faith is the same. Because of it, if I really take God's Word as true, then death is honestly not a big deal! My dad is with his Father in heaven. He has crossed that rainbow bridge. The same bridge I will cross soon. Saying soon isn't anticipating an imminent death but instead recognizes that the time I have here on earth is minuscule compared to the vastness of eternity.

Sitting there in that chair at the airport, God spoke to me plainly saying, "Don't respond as one without hope." I wanted my response to my dad's death to point people to the eternal reality. I wanted to glorify God through this tragedy.

As said before, hope is continually looking forward to heaven. Paul told us to "Rejoice in hope" (Romans 12:12). In other words, our joy comes from our hope. This makes a lot of sense. When we look forward to something, just the thought of it gives us joy.

As a child I would eagerly look forward to Christmas. My sister and I would sleep together in the same room on Christmas Eve. We would stir at about three in the morning and sneak into the living room lit by the colorful lights of the Christmas tree. Our stockings sat on the hearth of the fireplace, no longer hung with care. They were stuffed with goodies from Santa. This used to be my favorite memory of Christmas.

Of course my dad died a few days before Christmas. On Christmas Eve we sent the kids to bed. The adults stayed up busily wrapping presents and accomplishing in one evening what normally took all week. The family room of the house became Santa's workshop. Gifts were stacked up. Wrapping paper rolls were scattered, the remnants of which always seemed to hide the tape and scissors. Bowls of cereal mix were readily at hand. It tasted good, but seemed to fall short of my dad's recipe, which he would always make when our family gathered. We laughed and joked while we worked; this was a needed distraction from the events earlier in the week. This is now my new favorite Christmas memory.

If hope gives us joy, then it makes sense to figure out from where that hope comes. For most people, hope means little more than wishful thinking. "I hope I get that job. . . . I hope my team wins. . . . I hope I don't get in trouble." In any one of these sentences, the word *hope* could be replaced with the word *wish*.

As a child thinking about Christmas, I didn't just wish I would get presents. I knew I would.

Why?

Because I had gotten them every Christmas since I was born. My hope was built layer by layer from my experience year after year. I knew what would happen because it had happened so many other times.

The Bible calls this faith. Faith is trusting that something will happen because of what has already happened. I had faith that I would get presents because it had already happened. I had faith in my parents because they had already proven themselves good to me.

If hope is looking at the future, then faith is looking at the past and the present. In faith I look back and believe that Jesus rose from the dead. If He really came back from the dead, then that means He is God. That's nothing any human can do. If He is God, then that means His Word can be trusted. In it He says, "The one who believes in the Son has eternal life, but the one who refuses to believe in the Son will not see life" (John 3:36).

In the present I know God is good. If my parents, who are evil compared to God, can give me good gifts, then certainly God, who is holy, is giving me good gifts. Jesus knew this. He taught, "What man among you, if his son asks him for bread, will give him a stone? Or if he asks for a fish, will give him a snake? If you then, who are evil, know how to give good gifts to your children, how much more will your Father in heaven give good things to those who ask Him!" (Matthew 7:9–11).

My parents would never have wrapped up a rattlesnake for me to open on Christmas morning! Why then do we think God is doing that to us?

Seeing the past accurately allows us to trust God with the present. Seeing God in our present gives us hope for the future. Heaven isn't a mere wish. Instead it is the intersection of our faith and hope—past, present, and future coming together.

Hebrews 11:1 says it like this, "Now faith is the reality of what is hoped for, the proof of what is not seen." In other words, faith is living the eternal reality now. Living by faith is the only way to understand the world around us. Furthermore, it is the only way to find joy.

Faith gives understanding. Understanding provides hope. Hope produces joy.

28 MARIA'S STORY

In my life, faith gave understanding. Understanding provided hope; hope produced joy. I have witnessed the same in others' lives. Maria is one of those lives.

Maria lives on the floor below me in my South Bronx apartment building. Although I knew her, I didn't know her well before her daughter Chelsey died.

Maria told me the story of how her daughter died.

It was a hot July day. Maria and her family had spent a week barbecuing and swimming in her son's pool at his house in Long Island. As they drove back into the city via the Long Island Expressway, Maria was in the rear passenger-side seat of a forest green SUV. In front of her was her husband Joco. Next to him, driving, was her husband's best friend Carlos. Behind Carlos was Chelsey. Sitting between Maria and Chelsey in the backseat was Chelsey's friend Brandy. Chelsey and Brandy were best friends. Maria described the closeness of their friendship as "dirt under a nail."

Maria has no memory of what happened next. Her last memory was in the parking lot of Walmart. Her daughter was thrilled with her newly purchased blouses. They were walking to the vehicle, laughing and joking. Maria threw her cigarette to the ground before getting in the SUV.

This fond memory of Chelsey is filed in Maria's mind along with many others. Much like Joshua's grandfather, there seemed to be a filing cabinet of memories, except every file in Maria's mind has the name "Chelsey" blazoned across it in red, permanent ink.

For example, Maria remembers Chelsey's birth. Nearly everyone thought her baby would be a boy. Even the sonogram indicated a boy. Maria thought it was a mistake when they said, "It's a girl!" Joco, a former boxer with arms the size of barrels (Remember those arms? He was one of my "goons"!), cried as he held his tiny, little girl dressed in pink. The gentle giant was the only one who predicted their baby would be a girl.

Not expecting a girl, it took them some time to figure out a name. Finally they named her Chelsey Nicole. This was a name Chelsey never liked. As a teenager she would ask, "Why didn't you name me something more exotic?"

Chelsey was never one to keep her opinions to herself.

As teenagers do, she would get angry at Maria, telling Joco, "Um, look. You need to talk to your wife because she is getting on my last nerve. I can't deal with your wife anymore," as she shook a finger in the air.

It didn't take long for the tables to turn though. Angry at Joco, she would wave her whole hand in the air as she asked Maria, "Can you talk to your husband for me? I can't deal with your husband anymore."

Maria would respond, "But that's your father."

"My father—your fault!"

Of course a teenager's mood changes often. Whenever Chelsey wanted something, her tone changed as she would call to her father in a singsongy voice, "Papacito."

Joco would ask Maria, "What does your daughter want, and how much does it cost?"

Singing again, "Papa-ciiii-to."

Maria would jest, "Uh-oh Joco. You're in trouble. She sang it a little longer. It's expensive."

Chapter 28

All of these memories are vivid, easily pulled from the filing cabinet of Maria's mind. Yet she doesn't remember what happened after she threw her cigarette to the ground on the day that everything changed. Somebody told her what happened next.

On their way home the tire on the driver's side blew, causing Carlos to lose control of the vehicle. Weaving back and forth, Carlos tried to regain control but couldn't. The vehicle flipped, and flipped, and flipped.

Everyone had major injuries except for Joco. He was helped out of the car by good Samaritans. Carlos died after several unsuccessful attempts to revive him. Brandy couldn't move because her back was broken. Her foot was crushed as well. She remembers lying there and hearing Chelsey say, "Check mommy, make sure mommy's OK."

Maria was in a coma. She remembers waking up in the hospital and asking, "Where am I? Why am I here?" She cried out calling, "Hello? Hello?"

The lady next to her in the room ran out exclaiming to the nurses, "The lady's up! She's up! She's up!"

Maria's brain was significantly injured. Not in her right mind, she would yell at the nurses and curse at the doctors. Anyone who walked in the door was a target.

To make matters worse, she would pull the many life-supporting lines out of her body. Therefore the doctors sedated her for over three months, giving her brain time to heal.

Chelsey lived for several days after the accident. A comedian to the end, she lay in her hospital bed with nearly every bone broken saying, "My nail broke. You guys have to get my nails done. How does my hair look?"

She eventually died. Her funeral was held while Maria was still in a medically induced coma.

29 "GOD DOESN'T MAKE MISTAKES"

Maria's life was forever changed. Before the accident, she was as a workaholic, chain-smoking wife, mother, and grandmother who liked to read. She was equally proud of her daughter, sons, and her sons' grandkids. Maria and Joco would bristle with pride when their grandbabies walked through the door exclaiming, "Meema! Peepa!" They were Maria's special people.

Then there was the dancing. "Just call me the dancing queen," Maria would boast. With her five friends in tow, they would club hop their way across the city.

Her dancing days are but a distant memory. Now Maria was suffering from not only the physical effects caused by her brain injury, but the mental trauma and grief from her significant loss. The next several years included many doctor visits for Maria. As her body slowly recovered from a million and one health issues, some of her life began to get back to normal.

I began to see Maria more and more. Typically I would bump into her on the block in front of our apartment building. She would always stop to talk, not just with me but with just about everyone. Everybody knew her. Setting her walking cane to the side, she readily gave all she met a warm hug and a smile.

Her sadness was not as easily set aside. She carried it with her all the time. Feeling like a clown with a painted face, she would smile, joke, and laugh, but on the inside she was reeling from the loss of her daughter.

In her apartment Maria was surrounded by ghosts of her past, memories of precious moments with her daughter. She would walk to Chelsey's unchanged room and look at the dolls, bows, and bags Chelsey had collected. Sponge Bob sat prominently on the shelf with his big, cheesy grin. He was Chelsey's favorite.

Maria could almost hear Chelsey and Brandy's whispers. During slumber parties they would chat late into the night, only quieted by a knock on the door and Maria asking, "Would you girls go to bed, please?"

Maria's sadness and heartache seemed to intensify at night. She couldn't sleep. She sat on her couch at two in the morning letting the television watch her. Doctors prescribed sleeping pills and depression medication, but no pill could take away her pain.

Maria felt completely alone. She could be surrounded by a hundred people and feel as if she was the only one in the room. Even though she had her grandbabies, her boys, a wonderful husband, mom, and sisters, she felt she had nothing left.

Maria had never spent much time thinking about her Creator. She didn't even own a Bible. So when a doctor commented, "Thank God you made it!" she was puzzled. The thought that God saved her never crossed her mind. She had only asked God, "Why? Why did You give me this gift and take her away?"

Then one day a friend invited her to come to our ministry center named Graffiti 2.

Maria replied, "What's the name?"

"Graffiti 2."

"Come on! Graffiti 2?" Maria said to her friend.

"Yeah. I think you should come one day with me."

She didn't go on the first invitation.

Her friend invited her again, saying, "You need to get out of the house."

Maria simply replied, "I'll see."

Her response gradually changed from "No, no, no," to "I'll think about it," to "Maybe."

Her friend persisted, saying, "Just go once. Come with me once. Who knows, you might hear something, see something, feel something that is exactly what you need. If it's not for you, you don't ever have to come with me again."

Maria acquiesced, "OK. I'll go with you once."

On her first visit Maria felt an unfamiliar feeling—peace. Every time she went, she had the same feeling. It was the best feeling in the world. She knew she was home.

Maria's eyes were opened to her Author and Creator. She understood that He wasn't mean and vengeful but also He wasn't to be played with. She revered Him.

Seeing Him with new eyes, she also saw herself differently; she saw herself as a sinner. Her anger and temper didn't reflect His eternal glory. Her life before was built on her pleasure and her happiness. It now seemed so meaningless.

Maria began to understand the jealous love of her Heavenly Father, a patient jealousy that would draw her closer and closer to Him, a love that extended forgiveness. Forgiveness that was free to her, costly to Him.

Knowing her Author, finding her story in the pages of His story, Maria prayed, "Lord, only You can give me what I need: limitless, no price-tag, never-ending love."

Doctors restored Maria's life through medical care and treatment. But she says, "Doctor Number One" gave her a new, satisfying, eternal life.

Maria now sees everything differently. She views past, present, and future in light of the eternal truth. She has learned that truth by studying His Word.

Maria says, "Everything else is important: my mom, my family, my church, my spiritual family. They are all important, but my time with Him is first. It must come first. After that I can continue with the rest of my day."

Maria still struggles. She says, "I'm a work in progress. I don't know if *backslide* is the word to use. I don't fall to the point where I land. I kind of slide back a little and I'm like, "Father, you've got to get these thoughts out of my mind. You're the only one who can do this."

Maria knows she has an adversary. She describes him saying: "He's busy, busy, busy. The enemy works overtime. He attacks. He makes things happen in your life like the swelling of my feet. I've been to the doctors twice already. Do you know how many milligrams of medication I am on? Are you kidding?"

Then there are the temptations. Maria shared, "I used to smoke a lot. Now I can't be around cigarettes. I can't stand the smell. Not too long ago, I smelled one and thought. . . . *Hmm?*"

The smell drew her in.

Moments later she prayed, "Father, I need You to grab hold of me." The thought went away.

Focusing on her loss, sometimes she believes the enemy's lies and gets sad. Yet Maria now even looks at that part of her life differently. Not despite, but as a result of, the tragedy, Maria now confidently states, "God doesn't make mistakes."

That's faith! Although she doesn't fully understand the events of her past, her faith is helping her grow in understanding. As a result she has hope and that hope is producing joy.

She described her joy saying, "I do have joy. I just don't have that one thousand percent joy that I pray for. The peace that someday I know I will have."

Maria's sight isn't complete. There's nothing wrong with her eyes, but just like me her understanding can be foggy. Things are getting clearer for both of us. Clearer as we look to the end; clearer as we see with the eyes of faith.

CHAPTER

NOISY GONGS

BELOVED DAUGHTER AND SISTER
"A TRUE ANGEL ON EARTH"

Chelsey N Marin

4-13-1993 to 8-26-2011

MY DAD'S TOMBSTONE

JAMES PARKER MANN
CPT
US ARMY
VIETNAM

OCT 20 1943
DEC 19 2011

LOVING HUSBAND
FATHER AND PAPA

These two tombstones have one word in common (besides *and*): *love*. Chelsey was beloved. My dad loved.

The love of my father was readily apparent at his funeral as people lined up to share condolences with my family. My sister-in-law, Kristi, made the following observations on her blog, *Real Health, Wealth, and Happiness:*

> *While standing in line for Jim's showing I was struck by the number of people who came from all over the country and state to pay their respects to him. Person after person shared similar stories about Jim. He gave them a chance when no one else would, or he helped them with their horses, farms, houses, events, and more. There wasn't a single person who said they admired Jim's possessions, the long hours he worked, or his social status. Each person described how thankful he or she was for his service, genuine compassion, and for believing in him or her despite the cost or time for Jim. He shared his wealth unconditionally with them in whatever way he could. (realhwh.blogspot.com)*

At the conclusion of someone's life, little else matters. A person's career, education, failures, successes, or wealth don't carry much significance. What matters most is that they loved and were loved.

God's Word says the same thing. First Corinthians 13 says,

> *If I speak human or angelic languages but do not have love, I am a sounding gong or a clanging cymbal. If I have the gift of prophecy and understand all mysteries and all knowledge, and if I have all faith so that I can move mountains but do not have love, I am nothing. And if I donate all my goods to feed the poor, and if I give my body in order to boast but do not have love, I gain nothing.* (vv. 1–3)

In other words, a person can be multilingual, infinitely wise, supernaturally gifted, philanthropic, and seemingly able to accomplish the impossible. Without love, that person's life means nothing. At the end, nothing will be gained.

First Corinthians 13 goes on to discuss the qualities of true love. In a previous chapter we already made the observation that so many people settle for counterfeit love. This is not the love that comes from eternity but a cheap, valueless replica. The real thing is described as patient, kind, lacking envy, not boastful, not conceited, properly acting, unselfish, not provoked, grudge-less, believing the best is yet to come, weathering all things, trusting, and enduring (vv. 4–7).

Something I have come to understand is this: *Even on my best day my love falls short of this expectation.*

The day my dad had a seizure at the Thanksgiving table is an unfortunate, yet perfect example of this realization. I loved my dad. Seeing him have a seizure scared me so I reacted angrily. When he came out of the seizure, I screamed at him for not taking care of himself and going to the doctor. I don't remember what I said, but it certainly wasn't patient or kind.

Even though I loved him, I was unloving in my response. That's because my response was focused on me. If I were focused on my dad, I would have been patient and kind. I would have acted properly and not been easily provoked. I wouldn't have kept track of my dad's neglect of his health.

If then, at the end of life, not just the amount but also the quality of love given and received is the basis of determining the value of that life and ultimately what is gained from that life, I am in a hopeless predicament. The best love I have to offer falls far below the standard.

Jesus taught often about love. He summed up all of the law of the Old Testament by saying, "Love the Lord your God with all your heart, with all your soul, and with all your mind. . . . Love your neighbor as yourself" (Matthew 22:37–39).

Jesus said before we can love others we must first love God. If I were focused on God when my dad had the seizure at the Thanksgiving table, I would have been able to "bear all things, believe all things, hope all things, and endure all things" (1 Corinthians 13:7). I would have believed when things are out of my control, they are still in God's control.

If I were focused on God, I would have had Paul's confidence when he said, "We know that all things work together for the good of those who love God: those who are called according to His purpose" (Romans 8:28). Even when we don't understand what is happening, we can believed all things work together for our good, either now or eternally.

Such faith is rooted in God's love.

God's love is different than mine. His love doesn't meet the standard; it created the standard. Before I have any hope of loving in a similar way, I must first know that I am beloved by Him.

He loves me.

How much does He love me?

"But God proves His own love for us in that while we were still sinners, Christ died for us!" (Romans 5:8).

True love and sacrifice are always linked. Sacrifice is the fruit of love. Jesus said it like this, "No one has greater love than this, that someone would lay down his life for his friends" (John 15:13).

However, love is also a fruit of sacrifice. Now that I am older, I see how much my dad gave up for me. I understand better the depth of his love for me. In many ways, he sacrificed his own happiness for my happiness.

If I had eyes to see then what I see now, I definitely would have gone on more horseback rides with him. I would have spent more time in the barn. I definitely would have been more loving. When we know we are beloved, we respond with love. We want to be close to those who love us.

This feeling is magnified when we think about God's love. If we believe Jesus is God and He gave up His life for us, it is only natural we love Him. We therefore want to be close to Him.

There is nothing more valuable than loving God and being close to Him.

Ephesians 2:13 tells us how valuable it is to be close to God. "But now in Christ Jesus, you who were far away have been brought near by the blood of the Messiah." Being near to God is of incredible importance.

How valuable is it? It was worth Jesus' life.

Imagine I bought a person a Tic Tac. He or she might say, "Thank you." What would the person say if he or she found out I paid one million dollars for that Tic Tac?

How absurd! A Tic Tac isn't worth it.

What if I handed the Tic Tac to him or her with my left hand because I had cut off my right hand and traded it for that Tic Tac?

Now I'm just talking crazy, right? A Tic Tac isn't that valuable.

God places a value on me being close to Him. It is worth Jesus' life. If it's worth Jesus' life, it is certainly worth my life.

Love and sacrifice are connected not just here on earth, but eternally. We can't love God without sacrificing our lives. Just like Jesus did, we must willingly lay down our lives in order to pick up His life.

By doing so, not only will we love Him, but our lives will vibrate with the resonance of His love.

As a percussionist, I have played the gong and cymbals. I'm sure the instruments I have played aren't too different from the ones mentioned in 1 Corinthians 13 when it says that without love I am a "sounding gong or clanging cymbal."

On their own, these instruments are loud and obnoxious. So too are our lives without love. In the company of an orchestra, however, the gong and cymbal can provide the climactic punch to send the listener into musical bliss. Oh, the power of love!

A professional plays these instruments differently from an amateur. Amateurs simply hit the cymbal. It certainly makes a loud sound, but it lacks the depth and warmth of sound that a professional can draw from it.

A professional percussionist knows that the cymbal can be played in such a way to draw out its multifaceted overtones—these are sound waves the untrained ear doesn't readily hear, but they make the tone much better. To draw out these sounds, an experienced percussionist will warm up the cymbal. He or she will tap it lightly so it will begin to vibrate. Of course, the more it vibrates, the more the sound builds. The instrumentalist can then either create a sound that gradually washes over the listener, or a sound that hits the listener all at once.

For me, God has used the upside-down circumstances of life to tap on my soul. As a result of my dad's death, I began to better understand both of my fathers. I not only realized how much I was beloved by my dad but also how beloved I was by my heavenly Father. I vibrate with both my fathers' loves. No, not perfectly yet. But I no longer want God to stop tapping.

CONCLUSION

AUGUST 18, 2011

"Dad is in a mood. I still get so frustrated with him. It is hard to ignore. I don't know what to do to make the situation better."

I never dared to consider the struggles I experienced in my relationship with my father were shaping me into the man I would become. I now have a different perspective.

DECEMBER 19, 2011

"Andrew, something happened. . . . Your dad passed away."

There was a lot I didn't understand. However through his death, I began to understand the certainty of hope that sprouts from the root of faith.

AUGUST 27, 2012

"We found a mass. It looks like testicular cancer."

I never asked God to heal my soul. I didn't know I needed it. However, through cancer, the Great Physician brought more than just physical healing.

JULY 27, 2014

"For 16 years of my life, I have been disobedient. I need to be right before God and before my church. I need to be baptized."

I went from being a master of religion, concerned about what others thought, to being obedient to Jesus. I only cared what He thought!

CHAPTER

QUESTIONS

Encountering sin, sickness, struggle, and death leads us to ask questions. I have found in my life that questions are good. Questions lead to conclusions. Of course, to find the right conclusions, we need to ask the right questions.

Consider this: *What if the things I wrote about in this book never happened?* What if I didn't get baptized ten years after becoming a pastor? What if I never got testicular cancer? What if I didn't struggle in my relationship with my dad? What if my father hadn't unexpectedly died?

What if Ariel hadn't lived the messy life of a young urban male? What if Scott hadn't died of cancer? What if Joshua was born with normal brain function? What if Chelsey hadn't died as a result of a car wreck?

Simply put, there would be no book. I would not know the things I know now, and perhaps neither would you. Sin changed the way I think. Sickness taught me about healing, sin, and cancerous joy. Struggles have changed my perspective. Through death, I began to understand.

For all of the stories in the book, I can say the outcome of the sin, sickness, struggle, and death hasn't been loss, but gain. Struggle has brought newfound beauty to our stories.

Another question when facing difficult circumstances is, *Why?* Scott's wife asked that question after he passed away from cancer. Left with three kids to care for by herself, her confidence in Scott's eternity didn't relieve her immediate pressures.

Joshua's grandfather asked this question. He said, "A lot of kids are born with deformities—cleft palates, club feet—and you kind of accept those. In those cases there isn't any rationale behind any of it ever happening. It just happened. So you accept it. Unfortunately it happened to your child, but you still accept it. There's nothing you could have done differently. . . . With my grandson the situation should never have happened. You're constantly telling yourself what should have happened or what he should be. What he could have been. Why would this happen to him? Why did it happen to me?"

Hardly a day goes by that Maria doesn't ask, "Why did Chelsey have to die?"

Jesus didn't rebuke questions. He answered them. He often came to conclusions I never would on my own.

Jesus answered the question, *Why?*

Seeing a man born blind, Jesus' disciples inquired, "Rabbi, who sinned, this man or his parents, that he was born blind" (John 9:2). In other words they asked, *Why?*

Jesus responded, "Neither this man nor his parents sinned. . . . This came about so that God's works might be displayed in Him"(v. 3).

Why was this man blind? So God's work might be displayed. Jesus' response leads us to ask another question: *What is the work of God?*

The conclusion to this question can be found by reading the rest of the story. Jesus spit on the ground and rubbed the spitty, muddy dirt on the man's eyes. He instructed the man to wash himself in the pool of Siloam. The man came back to Jesus healed.

But that's not the end. That's not the final conclusion.

Jesus' encounter with the man planted a seed in his life that took root and grew. We see its rapid growth in the man's responses to the Pharisees' inquiries.

He first distances himself from Jesus, saying only, "He put mud on my eyes. . . . I washed and I can see" (v. 15).

He later steps further in faith calling Jesus a prophet.

It would have been easy for him to throw Jesus under the bus, to escape the Pharisees' judgment the third time when they demanded he call Jesus a sinner. Instead he boldly states, "Whether or not He's a sinner, I don't know. One thing I do know: I was blind, and now I can see" (John 9:25).

The outcome of all this—his blindness, healing, and trial—was evident when he says to Jesus, "I believe, Lord!" (v. 38).

Questioning isn't a faithless act. In fact, questioning God inherently contains the belief that there is something better than our current experience. Questioning God shows a belief that God is good and loving. Questioning helps us reconcile our current reality to the eternal reality. God uses questions and the circumstances of our life to grow our faith.

I remember from my childhood a painter on public television named Bob Ross. With palette in one hand and brush in the other, this soft-spoken artist with a larger-than-life, pillowy afro would paint a landscape right before my eyes. I never understood what he was doing as he was doing it. He would mix colors on his palette and then adeptly smear them across the canvas with his palette knife. Bright colors would be layered on dark colors. Sometimes it looked like he was totally covering up one color, leaving it unseen as he layered color upon color. It would all come together in the end as a beautiful work of art.

As I have experienced the upside-down circumstances of life—the sin, sickness, struggle, and death—I haven't been much different than I was as a kid watching Bob Ross paint. The hues, sometimes brushed smoothly, other times scraped jaggedly across my life, haven't always made sense.

I have learned that faith is believing an Artist of impeccable skill is painting a masterpiece. Each stroke of His brush is intentional across the canvas of our lives. Not all the colors are the same.

Ephesians 3:10 describes the Artist's "multifaceted wisdom." The word *multifaceted* could be translated as *multicolored*. These colors may seem random, dark, or out of place to me; they may be layered in ways that don't make sense to me; nevertheless, they are coming together to create something I don't have the perspective to see.

Faith is also realizing the Artist's canvas is much bigger than just my life. I have seen works of art that are made up of thousands of tiny pictures. They are called photomosaics. One example is a portrait of Abraham Lincoln composed of photos from the Civil War. In a photomosaic the whole is much greater than the sum of its parts. Each small picture matters, yet the small pictures don't tell the whole story. Too often it is easy to be consumed with each individual picture and fail to see the genius, the glory of the One who is bringing all these pictures together to display a masterpiece.

Faith is believing the Artist is in control of all the circumstances, working them together for our good, others' good, and ultimately His glory. A trip up the Hudson River along the Palisades in the fall displays the multifaceted brilliance of autumn leaves. Thousands of trees with millions of leaves, each leaf is beautiful, each tree is unique. Altogether, they create the beauty of fall.

But the beauty of fall isn't created by the effort of the leaves or the tree. It's created by the trees' environment, the external circumstances.

While I was in chemotherapy, I received the following poem about autumn leaves from a friend. This is the same friend who sent me to the church on the other side of the park filled with homeless people at the beginning of the book.

Yellow Leaves
By David Dean, October 26, 1998

Yellow leaves in the early morning sun
Reveal colors and texture totally blocked
By green chlorophylled leaves.

Why is it that the gorgeous hues of autumn
Emerge only when death for the leaf is imminent?

Green signifies the hard working photosynthesis factories
Hundreds, thousands on each tree—

Yet only when the activity slows and ceases
Do the rich yellows and reds of Fall
Brighten the forest and teach us a parable.

As I grow older and become aware of the cessation of some activity
I sense a new color emerging. Facing my own helplessness, I
Become aware of colors unknown when all was well.

As the pigments of my life change from the green of activity
Through the red of pain to the yellow of maturity
Brightened by the sunlight of your love . . .

Help me to surrender my heart to you, O Lord, and when the time comes
Help me to release my hold on this life and float effortlessly
On the wind of Your Spirit to my final resting-place.

This poem was written while recuperating from prostate surgery and in the midst of radiation treatments for prostate cancer. Every fall I am reminded of the mercy and grace of God as activity slows down.

God uses the sin, sickness, struggle, and death of our lives to change our color; they change the way we think. God doesn't force this on us, though; we have a part to play as well. We have to learn to listen and obey.

I'm not an artist. I can't draw or paint. One time I tried. I don't know what got into me. In my childhood one day after school I turned off *Full House,* went to the barn, picked up a can of spray paint, and painted a few white swipes across a little green yard wagon.

My dad later found it, and he wasn't happy.

To this day, my family still asks me, *Why?* I find it a little ironic all these years later that I work in a ministry with the word *graffiti* in its name.

Something I *can* do well is coloring a picture by number. I remember this activity from my childhood. A coloring page had a picture divided into sections. Each section had a different number, and each number was to be filled in with a different color. All the ones were supposed to be blue; all the twos colored red; all the threes filled in green, and so on.

A paint-by-number kit allows a person to create a beautiful masterpiece despite not having the skill of an artist; all he or she needs to do is follow the instructions.

If faith begins with believing an Artist is painting something better than we can, then our response is recognizing our life is much like that coloring page. We don't need to have the ability to paint; all we have to do is follow the instructions of the Designer.

In other words, we must trust the Designer's instructions, even when they don't make sense. When He says to paint the ones blue, we paint them blue. When He says to paint the twos red, we paint them red. When He says to paint the threes green, we paint them green.

In the end the finished work of art doesn't show off the ability of the one making the brushstrokes but instead shows the skill of the Designer.

32 LOSING CONTROL

All the events of my life have led me to the following conclusion: *Lord, not my will but Yours.*

That conclusion turns everything in life upside down. It is the result of changed thinking, spiritual healing, new perspectives, and deeper understanding. These things have given me a new mindset.

In my experience I have found it impossible to change my mindset on my own. Thoughts consume my mind that I just can't shake. A person's disapproving comment or my own awareness of my failure often linger like an unwelcome guest in my apartment.

It's comforting to know that Jesus struggled shaking His thoughts as well. The night of His betrayal, thinking about His upcoming crucifixion, He collapsed on the ground and pleaded, "My Father! If it is possible, let this cup pass from Me" (v. 39).

I wonder what He was dreading. Perhaps the thought of His imminent torture or the rejection of His friends overwhelmed Him. Whatever it was, He didn't ask just once or twice; He petitioned three times. He couldn't shake the thought!

With the weight of these thoughts bearing down on Him, each time Jesus came to the following conclusion: "Yet not as I will, but as You will" (Matthew 26:39).

Paul was a man who came to the same conclusion. Here is what he said, "Do not be conformed to this age, but be transformed by the renewing of your mind, so that you may discern what is the good, pleasing, and perfect will of God" (Romans 12:2).

We often think our circumstances aren't good, pleasing, or perfect. Therefore, we conclude, they are outside God's will.

Paul concludes that we will understand God's will when our mind is transformed, when we develop a new mindset. However, we can't just change our thinking on our own. The verse that comes before Romans 12:2 is crucial: "Therefore, brothers, by the mercies of God, I urge you to present your bodies as a living sacrifice, holy and pleasing to God; this is your spiritual worship" (v. 1). In other words, smash the idol of self.

When reading the Bible, I have learned to pay attention to words such as "so that" and "therefore." They indicate a conclusion has been made. Rarely can we come to the same conclusion if we don't see what came before.

To understand this verse and the reason for Paul's conclusion we have to read what comes before. This *therefore* is the conclusion drawn from twelve chapters of writing. The first half of the letter to the Romans explains the kingdom of God. Understanding God's kingdom alone though isn't enough; we must enter it.

Entrance into that kingdom requires a twofold sacrifice. Jesus didn't merely teach or exemplify life in God's kingdom; He created a pathway for us to live in His Father's kingdom. His sacrifice opened the doors to God's kingdom, but our sacrifice is how we enter. How do we present our bodies as a living sacrifice? Coming to the sincere conclusion, *Lord, not my will but Yours.*

All that Paul understood about God's kingdom led him to conclude God's kingdom is worth the sacrifice of his kingdom.

When he sacrificed his kingdom, his thinking changed. It turned his life upside down. Therefore, he urges us to do the same.

Life in this kingdom looks upside down from the world we know. Jesus explained it saying,

The poor in spirit are blessed, for the kingdom of heaven is theirs. Those who mourn are blessed, for they will be comforted. The gentle are blessed, for they will inherit the earth. Those who hunger and thirst for righteousness are blessed, for they will be filled. The merciful are blessed, for they will be shown mercy. The pure in heart are blessed, for they will see God. The peacemakers are blessed, for they will be called sons of God. Those who are persecuted for righteousness are blessed, for the kingdom of heaven is theirs. You are blessed when they insult and persecute you and falsely say every kind of evil against you because of Me. Be glad and rejoice, because your reward is great in heaven. For that is how they persecuted the prophets who were before you.
(MATTHEW 5:3–12)

Jesus said the deflated not the inflated, the grieved not the calloused, the soft not the hard, the cravers of good not those satiated with pleasure, the gracious not the retaliatory, the undivided not the hypocrite, the reconcilers not the dividers, the afflicted not the easy-living are blessed.

They are happy.

They are joyful because they live eternally minded rather than worldly-minded. They focus on God's good rather than their good. They don't stand on their own pedestals. They trade their kingdom for God's.

Although I don't drive often, driving in the city has changed how I drive. Survival in New York City requires a little more assertiveness—in all areas of life, but especially while driving. When I return to Missouri, habits die hard. My city driving isn't easily turned off. This often concerns my mom; her concern is given a voice when she yelps, pushes her foot into the floor, and grabs my arm. I always say, "Mom,

I saw the brake lights!" Even when they catch me off guard, I rarely admit it.

One time I was glad my mom wasn't in the car. The hubris of youth caused me to have a heavy foot as I drove the thirty-mile trek into town from our farm. It was raining. Between the swipes of my windshield wipers squeaking back and forth, I saw the brake lights of a stopped car waiting to turn ahead. I slammed on my brakes, but the wet ground caused me to hydroplane. I was out of control. My car fishtailed and turned as I glided across the pavement. I came to a stop on the shoulder, facing the opposite direction, parallel to the car I had moments earlier been careening toward. I was saved, certainly not by any James Bond ability of my own.

Jesus taught that living in our kingdom is much the same. We may think we are in control, but we're not. All it takes is something disastrous for us to realize we need help. We need to be saved. We can't save ourselves.

Jesus said He came to save us. He told Nicodemus this in what is likely the most familiar verse from the Bible, "For God loved the world in this way: He gave His One and Only Son, so that everyone who believes in Him will not perish but have eternal life" (John 3:16). We must believe we need saving and that Jesus is our Savior. Sin, sickness, struggle, and death have a knack of bringing us to this conclusion. As our Savior, He saves us from living for ourselves within our own kingdoms. By His sacrifice we become children of God, participants and heirs in His kingdom.

Jesus though isn't merely our Savior, He must also be our Lord. That means we give up control, listen to Him and obey Him. As our Lord, Jesus teaches us to live every moment with that kingdom in mind—to live life upside down.

Jesus understood these principles. He lived in His Father's kingdom. As a result on that night when He couldn't shake his thoughts, He finally concluded, "Yet, not as I will, but as You will" (Matthew 26:39).

So He got up and said, "Let's go!" (Matthew 26:46).

The next few days must have been horrid. He was betrayed by His friends, shamed as leaders spit in His face, beat again and again, and ultimately hung on a cross to die.

Moments before that death, He exclaimed, "*Tetelestai.*—It is finished" (John 19:30). Then He bowed His head and yielded the only thing He had left. He gave up His spirit. He died.

It was finished. The work of salvation was done.

That's not how others saw it. They saw failure. They saw defeat. They saw death.

However, failure was victory. Defeat was exaltation. Death was life.

You may not see it now, but wait a few days, you'll see!

33 COMPLETE JOY

Jesus knew upside-down living would not come easy to us. That's why he spent so much time teaching about God's kingdom. He wanted us to experience eternal satisfaction, to experience joy. He said, "I have spoken these things to you so that My joy may be in you and your joy may be complete" (John 15:11).

The word *complete* means "lacking nothing." Our tendency is to think we aren't happy because something is missing from our life. We think, *If I could only have . . . If this were better . . . If I had just a little more . . . then I would be happy.* Life becomes one big puzzle where we are always looking for the missing piece.

Jesus' description of joy is one that is not looking for anything else because it is lacking nothing. This life lacks nothing because it has found all it needed in a relationship with God through Jesus. That means needing nothing besides Him.

Through the years I have thought I needed many things to make my life better, happier, and more complete. I thought I needed people's approval; I thought I needed to save Ariel; I thought I needed relief from my hiccups; I thought I needed a better relationship with my dad; I thought I needed to resolve my dad's loose ends from his business.

Ariel described the struggle in his life from not having a father. He thought he needed a father.

Joshua's grandfather thought he needed Joshua's love. He felt a sense of completeness from Joshua. He described it saying, "You think about what brings you joy in the world: food, Broadway shows. There's no joy like rocking my grandson every night. Looking at him and him looking at me, it's like there's nothing else in the entire world. Just he and I. That's all there is."

What will happen, though, when Joshua is gone?

Maria knows. Chelsey is already gone.

Looking back, Maria says, "I realize that my whole life was all about my girl, my baby. My world revolved around her. If she coughed, I took her to the emergency room. I was obsessed. The Lord was like, 'OK, you've forgotten about Me.'"

Jesus never forgot about His Father and He taught us to do the same. This teaching comes right before He talks about complete joy in John 15. Jesus calls God a Gardener, describes Himself as the Vine, and us as the branches. The outcome of a life of faith is fruit. Jesus wants us to live a faithful life so His joy will be in us and our joy may be complete.

The picture Jesus paints in His teaching is a life that is complete, lacking nothing, because of the relationship a person has with God through Jesus.

Jesus is key. Here's the reason: There is no joy without hope; there is no hope without knowing the end; we can't know the end because we don't know what happens after death; but Jesus does!

Without Jesus we are incapable of hopeful living because we have never experienced eternity. Jesus has. He is eternal. He's the Vine. We must be connected to Him, not a person, not a church—Jesus. His roots are in heaven; yet He's lived our reality. So when Jesus says, "Remain in me" (John 15:4), He is saying, "Rather than dig your roots in the soil of this world, grow out of Me, the One rooted in eternity."

Jesus doesn't tell us to grow out of Him without telling us how. He tells us, "If you keep My commands you will remain in My love, just as I have kept My Father's commands and remain in His love" (John 15:10).

It's not instinctive for us to connect the word *love* with the word *command*. Often the most commanding people don't seem that loving. However, love and truth are linked.

Not far from where I live in the Bronx is St. Jerome's Church. The green patina on the bronze spires of this church often come in and out of view as I walk our streets. When it was built in the late 1800s it was the place of worship for the many Irish parishioners who lived in the neighborhood. Today, its worshippers are reflective of the many Mexicans who have moved into the community.

A statue sits at the corner of the church. I assume it is St. Jerome. The placard is engraved with this statement: "Love without truth is just sentimental; truth without love is sterile."

During my years of ministering in the Bronx, I have tried to grow in my ability to share both love and truth. It's definitely not easy.

My dad was pretty good at balancing the two. Often I would only focus on his critiques, the truth he had to share with me. However, he was loving.

One of the most unsettling times of my life was my first week at New York University. My parents and I flew to New York on a Friday. We toured the city, and my parents helped settle me in on Saturday. On Sunday they left. I felt alone.

I wasn't alone, though. I was in a dorm room with four others. My roommates and I formed a virtual United Nations. One was from Spain; another was from Taiwan; a third from Singapore; and the last from South Korea. Then of course, I was from Southeast Missouri. As eclectic as we were nationally, we were also diverse in lifestyle. This small-town, Christian boy moved into a dorm where a bucket of condoms was always sitting just inside the resident assistant's door.

It was overwhelming at first. I felt like I was sinking.

Then came a message. It was a voice message on my phone.

My phone rang during an orientation meeting, but I was unable to pick it up. Stepping into the hallway later, I listened to the message. It was my dad. With choked-up words, evidence of the unseen tears in his eyes, he said, "Andrew, your mom and I miss you. Hope everything is well. We love you."

I played that message over and over again. Those words were so valuable to me. They demonstrated the love of my father.

Our eternal Father has a message of love as well.

He says, "I love you."

Equally important, though, is the truth: "You're a sinner."

If God told us the truth without love, we would be left to our own consequences. We would live in constant fear of damnation. If God loved us without telling us the truth, we would obliviously live carefree lives, but our happiness would all come to an end with our physical death.

God held both truth and love in his hands and hung them on the nails of the Cross. When we accept the truth, and know His love our reward is joy, eternal satisfaction.

Eternal satisfaction isn't just in the age to come, but now. God's commands are His truths to be enacted now. He loves us and wants us to be happy. He knows things we don't, so even when His commands seem upside down to us, we can trust he is looking out for our good.

I don't expect my dog, Proof, to understand why I give her commands, but I do expect her to be obedient. Of course, she had to learn how to be obedient. Proof came from a training program in Kansas. Prior to our meeting, she spent nearly a year being trained. When her training was complete, I flew to Kansas, and we spent a week together getting to know each other.

Now, there's at least 50 commands she obeys. *Sit! Down! Take a break* (means go to the bathroom)! *Roll over! Go to heal! Get it! Bring it! Hug!* There's many more. She always responds. Well, most of the time. As she ages, she is becoming slightly like the little, old *viejas* (old women) in our neighborhood—just a little stuck in her ways!

I don't expect Proof to respond to my commands because I am on a power trip. I expect her to because I love her. There will always be things I know which she doesn't. The commands I give based on the truths I know, some of which she will never know, are for her own good.

At the end of our week of training in Kansas, Proof and I went to a mall to take a public-access test. Passing this test would allow me the right to have Proof with me in public places. The test included rolling a ball in front of Proof as well as the other dogs being tested. Some chased after the ball. Proof was obedient to my *stay* command. When a large cookie tray was slammed to the ground, startling many spectators, Proof remained calm. As we walked around the mall, knowing we were being watched, I was paying attention to the smallest detail of what I had been taught earlier in the week.

My focus was interrupted when a woman asked, "Can I pet your dog?" Service dogs are not allowed to be petted in public. Before I could respond, the woman was on the floor, sitting cross-legged. Proof nuzzled close. The woman began petting Proof as Proof plopped down beside her, and I watched nervously for any grading onlookers.

My anxiety was washed away by the woman's tears. They were running down her face.

I looked closer at her as Proof began licking her weathered hands. The dishevelment of her life was apparent by her worn clothes and wrinkled, leathery face.

She sat with Proof for five or six minutes.

With what seemed like a new sense of resolve, the woman eventually stood and took a few steps away. She paused, looked at Proof, turned back to me, and said, "That dog is proof God exists."

Proof is just a dog. Yet she glorified God simply by existing. She didn't glorify God through any extraordinary effort. She glorified God simply by being and doing what she was created to be and do—nothing more, nothing less.

Oh, the simplicity of obedience! Obedience is being and doing what God has created us to be and do.

So often we concern ourselves with the doing over the being. Doing without being has consequences. First, our anxiety rises when we are more concerned about doing than being. As doers, we have limited time to complete seemingly infinite responsibilities. As be-ers, we have infinite time to complete only what our Father wants us to do.

Second, doers *might* gain the whole world, but they *will* lose their soul. How horrifying it would be to hear from Jesus, "I never knew you! Depart from Me" (Matthew 7:23).

Combined, these two consequences destroy the possibility for complete joy. Not only is eternal joy impossible, but temporary pleasure is fleeting as well.

Before I can *do* in a way that glorifies God, I must first *be*. What must I be? I must be a child of God. I must be a part of His kingdom. I must be attached to the Vine. I must be alive by His Spirit.

If I'm not, the end is bleak. Jesus warns us about this in His teaching: "If anyone does not remain in Me, he is thrown aside like a branch and he withers. They gather them, throw them into the fire, and they are burned" (John 15:6).

Every fall when I was a child, my brother, sister, and I would collect the dead branches around our yard. We would put them into a pile and burn them. Oh, how I loved that smell!

Jesus says the Gardener does the same thing with dead branches. They are gathered and burned. Sometimes it's obvious when something is dead, like when I was a kid burning branches. Other times it's not so obvious.

A few years ago I was in Central Park enjoying a Memorial Day picnic. The calm of the day was interrupted by a disturbing sound. It was a crack, followed by leaves rustling, then a loud thump. Not too far from us the branch of a gigantic elm had fallen. To our horror the picnic goers beneath the tree were now under the heavy branch.

People rushed to their aid. Although no one was killed, several people were hurt.

The lesson from this experience and from Jesus' teaching is, *We may look like we are alive, but we may be dead.*

Consider Judas. We know him as the betrayer, but to all those around him, Judas was a disciple. From his life we're reminded that it's possible to look like a disciple, talk like a disciple, but not be a disciple.

Judas was more concerned with what Jesus could do for Him than who Jesus was. His life definitely didn't end with joy. His dissatisfaction led to his suicide.

It's easy for me to focus more on what Jesus can do for me than who Jesus was. A similar mindset is to be more concerned with what I can do for Jesus than who I am. Both result in dissatisfaction—longing for something more.

In the end, what I do doesn't matter, it's who I am in relation to Jesus. Am I connected to the Vine? Am I a child of God?

Only by knowing Jesus can I know who I truly am. Only by knowing Jesus can I live life lacking nothing. Only by knowing Jesus can I have complete joy.

34 URBAN FARMING

The kingdom of heaven is like a mustard seed that a man took and sowed in his field. It's the smallest of all the seeds, but when grown, it's taller than the vegetables and becomes a tree, so that the birds of the sky come and nest in its branches (MATTHEW 13:31–32).

So much of Jesus' teaching about the kingdom of God involved farming. Although I live in the city now, farming isn't foreign to me. Growing up in rural Missouri, I had various farm chores like mowing the yard, mucking out the stalls, and feeding the horses.

My first paying job was in middle school. I worked on a soybean farm. My job was to drive the bean truck. Most of the time I would just sit around while the farmers in the tractors planted the beans. But when those tractors ran out of beans, I would drive the old truck to them and help fill up the bean hoppers.

Here are three simple farming principles I know: (1) The seed looks different from the fruit; (2) The fruit comes later; and (3) The fruit is more abundant than the seed.

First consider the difference between the seed and the fruit. All a person needs to do is cut open an apple to see the seed and fruit look nothing alike. So many of the truths that now give me the greatest joy were sewn in times of difficulty, defeat, and even depression. Without my struggle with sin, I wouldn't know the gospel—that God saves sinners like me. Had I not been diagnosed with testicular cancer, I would have found no cancerous joy. God has used these circumstances to do what I could never do on my own: *Change the way I think!*

Then consider the timing of the harvest. The harvest isn't immediate. It comes later, sometimes much later. Remember, I mentioned that Joshua's grandfather marveled at what he learned in his embryology class? The formation of a human from a mass of cells still amazes him decades later. How anything grows is truly astounding!

Understanding these principles has helped me to minister in the Bronx. One of the ways we help our neighborhood is by coaching adults to prepare for their high school equivalency diploma. Many of these individuals have found themselves shackled by previous choices in their lives. They have often chosen friends, girls, or weed. Their decisions make sense when a person is building their own kingdom. After all, if life is temporary, immediate pleasure makes more sense than long-term gain.

Sometimes these guys regret their decisions. Sometimes they are unaware of the consequences. Either way, I often see them make the same short-term choices all over again. They want to do algebra before they know their multiplication tables. They want to write an essay before they can write a sentence. Not to mention the fact they continue to choose friends, girls, and weed.

I find myself praying, "God, change the way they think."

Such change often takes a long time. Not too long ago the increasing violence of our neighborhood broke my heart for several young men. I began praying for them.

Early one morning while I quietly worked in my office, one of these young men came and sat on our couch. I had known him for ten years. I also had close connections to the family he had a "beef" with, as they call it in our neighborhood. He was the reason my friend lay in the hospital bed the night I was called to the hospital.

Sitting next to him on the couch, I put my hand on his shoulder and said, "It's good to see you. What's up?"

He replied, "I need help."

He began talking about how he needed to shape up his life. He had wanted to come and ask for help before but knew I was close friends with his rivals.

We had a blunt conversation. He said he was ready to walk a different direction, so he attended our high school equivalency preparation class the next day. Unfortunately, within a week he was no longer coming. He wanted to change his outcome so he changed his actions.

Yet he hadn't changed his thinking, but seeds have been planted. A previous book in the "Upside-Down" series talks about snow building on a roof until it collapses (*Upside-Down Devotion,* page 114). It's hard to think the weight of one snowflake could do a roof in. Yet at some point one more snowflake is the breaking point. This isn't always a devastating outcome. The circumstances of our life sometimes have to pile up until the roofs of our kingdoms collapse and we change the way we think.

When this happens, the fruit is always more abundant than the seed. Farming only makes sense if the outcome is greater than the investment. After all, seed is expensive. Farmers know costly seed will yield great reward later. The reward is the fruit.

Fruit is produced as a result of what something is. For example, an apple tree produces apples. A pear tree produces pears. The same is true in the kingdom of God. The fruit of our life is the result of what we are, not what we do.

If we are children of God, heirs of His kingdom, attached to the Vine, then we will produce fruit.

Neither the branch nor the tree labors at fruit production. Two factors determine the quality and quantity of fruit: external circumstances (sunlight, water, pests, and soil conditions) and the work of the gardener.

The external circumstances of our life are the sin, sickness, struggle, and death we encounter. Never would I have wanted the circumstances for myself or the others I wrote about in this book. Yet, for all of us, they have shaped who we are today. For me and many others, they have opened our eyes to God's kingdom. As our eyes have opened, not only have we wanted to open them wider, but as Ariel said, "We want to open others' eyes as well."

God wants to do the same using sin, sickness, struggle, and death. In John 15 Jesus described His Father as the Master Gardener. The work of this Master Gardener produces abundant fruit.

I remember in my childhood my father cutting the forsythia bush. The first time I saw him prune the bush, I didn't understand why he cut it back to almost nothing. It looked horrible to me. Later in the season, though, it blossomed. It was beautiful.

We must remember the kingdom of God doesn't work the way we expect. It's almost always upside down from the way we would do things. The greatest opportunity for the Master Gardener to show His skill is through the devastating circumstances of life. He's able to make the best of these circumstances for the benefit of His garden.

Looking back in my life, I clearly see God using the struggle. He's used it in all the stories I have told.

Sometimes people expend a lot of effort trying to avoid struggle. Knowing how God worked in my life though, I have to believe God can use even the worse of circumstances for their good and His glory. Perhaps we should spend less time helping people avoid struggle and instead help them find the Gardener, Artist, Author, Creator, God in the midst of struggle.

Struggle provides opportunity, so rather than avoid it, use it as an opportunity to grow in love for God and help others do the same.

We work in our lives to avoid struggle, but Jesus gravitated toward it. He didn't avoid the lepers, the prostitutes, or the tax collectors. He seized every opportunity to enlist them in His Father's kingdom.

Living this way is anything but easy, primarily because we are ineffective at seeing the conclusion, the outcome, the fruit of our labors.

We often see the world through the lenses of cause and effect. One thing causes another to happen. Of course, this is true, but we are not good judges of what the cause or effect is.

In my early years of ministry in the city, one thought weighed heavy in my mind. Over the years I had formed many relationships with a lot of young guys in both Chicago and New York City. Most people would look at their circumstances and deem them failures. In my darker hours I didn't think they were failures; I thought I was. I would think: *What did I do? What did I not do? What could I have done differently?*

God spoke to me powerfully one night several years after beginning ministry in the Bronx. I was back on the Eisenhower Expressway outside Chicago. I had spent a fun day in the city reuniting with a bunch of the guys from the old Bible study.

Neither I nor anyone else would look at the surface of their lives and deem them ministry successes. Two had spent some time in jail, and one already had a baby with his girlfriend.

They all smoked weed and drank liquor, although not with me. Remember, no matter what the Riker's prison officers think, I'm not a weed-smoking pastor!

In my car, nearly alone on the ten-lane expressway, I was talking with God.

"I feel like I never should have left. I feel like I abandoned them. Their lives could have been different."

God spoke to me inaudibly but plainly: "Andrew, you're not their God; I am. I love them more than you do."

I am not the cause of anything. God is the cause of all things!

We are also poor judges of the effect. Just because I don't see the effect doesn't mean it isn't there.

God was and is working in all the lives named on the list in my mind. He is working in their lives the same way He has worked in mine, through sin, sickness, struggle, and death.

But God is also working in their lives in another way. It's one of the ways God has worked in my life. He's worked through influential people. Just as I can make a list of my failures, I can also make a list of men and women who have impacted my life. Some of them may not even know they are on the list.

When I was young, a little after the age at which I drew the picture of my mansion, I had an epiphany. Here it is: *Nothing is more valuable than changing one single life. For that life, that's everything. For every life that life changes, it's everything.*

I have always loved the old story of a boy walking the coastline. He comes up on a huge pile of starfish. Washed ashore and abandoned by the tide, the outcomes for these starfish look bleak.

A man, also walking the coastline, sees the boy. He is puzzled by what he sees the boy doing.

The boy is picking up the starfish one at a time and throwing them back in the ocean. The man gently chides the boy cynically saying, "What are you doing? You can't save all those starfish. There's too many of them!"

Without any pause the boy picks up another starfish and says, "No, I can't save them all, but I can save this one." He hurls that blessed starfish back into the ocean. For *that* starfish, nothing was more valuable.

I know I may not be the cause, but what a blessing to know that God is working through my life. I may not know the conclusion or outcome, but that's OK. I am time-bound. Part of being God's child is sacrificing my timeline. After all, He is eternal. He's not time bound, so He has all the time of eternity to accomplish exactly what He wants to do—both in and through a person's life.

Often the effects of our efforts are imperceptible. At our ministry center in the Bronx, I remind others and myself that the work we are doing often takes years and decades to see results. We may not see the change in a person's life from one day to the next.

Rarely are giant leaps taken. Instead, change takes place one step at a time. That's how plants grow. Works of art are completed one brushstroke at a time. Stories are written one letter, one word, one sentence, one paragraph, one page, one chapter, one book, one volume at a time.

I saw some of this story unfold at our ministry center. Although Manhattan is more of an epicenter for homelessness, it isn't uncommon for me to encounter a homeless individual in the Bronx. Christine is one of these women. When I first met her, I couldn't help but notice two teeth. They were the only two teeth visible in her mouth. They stuck out of her mouth like the teeth of a saber-toothed tiger. On a later visit I noticed she didn't have these teeth any more.

On a rainy, fall day I was in the office attending to the more mundane duties of my job while a few women waited outside my door to help unload a food delivery that was on its way. One of these women was Maria. Christine walked in and sat on our black, leather couch. I took a break from my to-do list and sat with her. The odor of urine was strong. As we talked, I noticed her feet. She had on sandals with no socks.

Although this wasn't a particularly cold day, I knew many cold days were ahead, so I asked her shoe size. She responded, "8 ½ or 9." I told Christine, "I don't have any shoes here, but I will see if I can find some by next week."

I knew Christine was hungry, so I excused myself to get her some food to eat from our pantry. I was stopped by Maria before I reached the stairs that descended to the basement toward the pantry.

Maria said, "Andrew, I have a closet full of clothes, a drawer full of socks, and so many shoes."

I knew she was talking about her daughter's room, the room she hadn't touched for three years since Chelsey passed away.

"Chelsey wore an 8 ½ or 9."

God was prompting Maria. She knew that none of this was coincidence.

In her mind she heard Chelsey saying, *What are we going to do with all these clothes? I'm not wearing them. We need to give them to someone who can use them.*

"Andrew, I need to go home to get some things for Christine."

Maria left. I got some granola bars and vanilla pudding and gave them to Christine. She ate them on the couch as I went back to my duties.

I worked on a project, had a meeting, and made some phone calls. I kind of forgot about Christine.

Then the food delivery we had been awaiting arrived. Several of my coworkers and volunteers began unloading the van. It was full of produce from Amish farmers in Pennsylvania—apples, peppers, pumpkins, eggplant, green beans, potatoes, and cabbage. As I carried a box around the corner, I saw Maria.

Maria was sitting next to Christine, bending over. With Chelsey's sock in hand, she pulled it over Christine's calloused foot. She then took Chelsey's shoe and gently slid it on over the sock. Christine smiled a toothless grin.

Maria offered a hug saying, "Hugs are free. You can have as many as you want."

Although I don't see or understand perfectly, I believe that had Chelsey not died, Maria would not have had this opportunity, and Christine would not have felt Maria's warm embrace.

God is working. He's working in Maria's life. He's working through her life. He's working in Christine's life. He's even working through Christine's life (after all, she has made the pages of this book). He's a Master Gardener. Upside-down things like this happen in His kingdom.

Oh the joy in watching the story unfold and praising the Author who is accomplishing more than I can possibly imagine!

CHAPTER

35 KINGDOM PLANTING

When something makes me happy, I always want to share it with someone, often my mom. I have no shame in saying, "I'm a momma's boy!" When I have a new idea, a changed way of thinking, it never makes sense to keep it to myself; I tell someone.

I have found satisfaction and eternal joy from living in relationship with Jesus, living with the end in mind, and living in God's kingdom. I want the same happiness for others. Therefore, I find ways to tell them.

Jesus was eternally satisfied, and He wanted the same for us. Do you remember His announcement at the beginning of His ministry? "The time is fulfilled, and the kingdom of God has come near. Repent and believe in the good news!" (Mark 1:15).

Jesus didn't just talk a good talk. He walked the walk. He planted seeds of the kingdom of God in the lives He encountered.

To plant seeds of God's kingdom, Jesus first met people's needs. He lived with, taught, fed, and healed people. Often these needs were the result of sin, sickness, struggle, and death. He found opportunity in people's struggles. As He met their needs, He taught about His Father's kingdom. Doing these two things together, He lifted their eyes from their short-term, temporary circumstances and opened them to the truth of eternity and who He truly was.

He told people that entrance into God's kingdom involved changed thinking (repenting) and faith (believing in the good news).

As a result of His ministry, people believed. They put their faith in Him as their Savior and Lord.

Peter is an example. Jesus asked Peter, "Who do you say that I am?" Simon Peter answered, "You are the Messiah, the Son of the living God!" (Matthew 16:15–16).

Jesus responded to Peter's profession with a powerful statement: "And I also say to you that you are Peter, and on this rock I will build My church, and the forces of Hades will not overpower it" (v. 18).

Jesus built the church on faith. What He builds even hell can't conquer!

Jesus' death, resurrection, and ascension secured the victory for the church. Although He is no longer physically present in the world, He is present in believers' lives through His Spirit, and He is present in the world through His church.

He described the church as agents of His kingdom: "I will give you the keys of the kingdom of heaven, and whatever you bind on earth is already bound in heaven, and whatever you loose on earth is already loosed in heaven" (v. 19).

As His agents, the church prays and seeks what Jesus prayed, "Your kingdom come. Your will be done on earth as it is in heaven" (v. 10).

So how do we plant the kingdom here on earth?

We do what Jesus did.

We begin with ministry. Ministry plows the ground for planting seeds. *Ministry* is simply defined as "meeting needs." God works in and through our lives to meet our needs and the needs of those around us.

People have different types of needs. A psychologist named Abraham Maslow described human needs with a pyramid: *Physiological needs* are on the bottom of the pyramid. These include breathing, food, water, and sleep. *Safety needs* are next. Safety involves security of body, resources, family, and health. *Love and belonging* are on the next level. Friendship, family, and community are integral at this level. Second from the top is *esteem*. Esteem is composed of confidence, achievement, respect of others, and respect by others. Sitting at the top is *self-actualization*. This deeper level of need includes morality, creativity, and lack of prejudice.

If ministry if plowing the soil, it's helpful if we use two hands. The two hands of ministry are relief and release. In previous book in this series, Taylor Field described relief work as the "immediate response to need" (*Upside-Down Devotion*, page 175). This type of ministry meets needs at the bottom of the pyramid. "Relief work is the simple act of giving someone a sandwich, no questions asked. Relief work hands a cold person a coat, or gives them a mattress to sleep on."

One day early in my experience of living and ministering in the Bronx, I was walking to the grocery store and saw a crowd of people. As I walked closer I saw a man unconscious on the ground. His face was blue. I had recently received CPR training but never thought I would actually use it.

I reached for my breathing barrier, which I had worn on a lanyard around my neck since my training. It wasn't there. I paused, looked at the man's arms, and saw holes dotted with blood. He was a heroin addict.

I didn't feel safe giving him CPR, but I didn't feel right not doing CPR. I thought, *Is my life more valuable than his?*

Then I remembered across the street sat a tent. Several days each week, condoms and clean needles were distributed from below a red awning with the words *Harm Reduction Center* written in white.

I yelled across the street, "Do you have a breathing barrier?"

They did. Someone brought it to me.

I placed the clear plastic over the man's cold, blue lips and began puffing breaths of air into his lungs.

His chest rose. Then it sank.

Time passed as I breathed over and over again. Eventually paramedics arrived.

On their cue, I stopped and removed the breathing barrier.

The man looked better. Color had returned to his face, but he still lay unconscious.

The paramedic took a look at him, grabbed him by the shoulders, shook him, and yelled, "Wake up!"

The man jumped to his feet!

All I could think was, *They didn't teach me that technique in CPR training!*

What if I had walked up to the man lying on the ground and started lecturing him about drug use? The man would have died. At that moment there was one thing he needed, air. Relief work provides a person what they need now, their earthly needs, so later we can provide what they will need for all eternity.

Release work meets needs on the higher levels of the pyramid. A previous book in the "Upside-Down" series described this type of work: "Release work also helps set people free from destructive habits, addictions, defeating behaviors, and stinking thinking. Release work often has an immediate component, and a component that takes much longer" (*Upside-Down Devotion*, p. 176).

Several years ago I met a man playing basketball in the park. This older gentleman was a regular sight each morning as I walked past the park on my way to our ministry center. We would exchange friendly greetings and small talk. Then I would go my way, and he would take a few more shots at the basket.

After years of this shallow routine, I thought, *I need to get to know this man better.*

We went to lunch. As we talked, he often said, "I'm a shy guy," but he kept talking and opening up. He had lived in our neighborhood for many years. He had countless stories from years gone by. These weren't good years in our community.

I enjoyed getting to know him, and he enjoyed getting to know me. Most of all, my new friend had an opportunity to get to know

God. He placed his faith in Jesus and subsequently got baptized the same day as me!

Then my friend disappeared. I didn't know what happened until a month later I saw him riding his daughter's bike down the street toward our ministry center. He looked a little silly, sitting on a tiny, pink bike, with his legs nearly up to his chest.

His face looked fresh and bright.

He told me, "I checked myself into rehab but now I'm back."

During all of our previous conversations, we had never talked about his struggles with alcohol. They were obvious. That was not a problem I could fix, but God could. God did. God changed his thinking. My friend was released.

We never know what God is doing.

As I sat with my friend eating lunch that day several months before, he said something unexpected.

"I saw you that day."

"What day?"

"The day you brought that man back to life in front of the grocery store."

I couldn't believe it. I didn't even know him then. He saw and remembered. The air I gave to the man on the ground later brought air to the soul of my new friend. The relief work had an unexpected outcome. It planted the seed of release. The fruit would come much later, nearly ten years later.

Ministry involves both relief work and release work. Sometimes we never know the outcome of the work we do.

As we do relief and release work, we need to remember to minister well. We shouldn't just do something; we should do the right thing well. This always involves living with integrity, taking care of yourself, and treating people with dignity.

Ministry can take place anywhere. However, if Jesus is our example, His words in John 20:21 must be considered. He said, "As the

Father has sent Me, I also send you." At the beginning of Luke, Jesus tells us what the Father sent Him to do: "He has anointed Me to preach good news to the *poor*. He has sent Me to proclaim freedom to the *captives* and recovery of sight to the *blind*, to set free the *oppressed*, to proclaim the year of the Lord's favor" (Luke 4:18–19). He was sent to minister to those in need—the poor, captives, blind, and oppressed. He didn't do that from afar. In Eugene Petersen's *The Message*, John 1:14 says, "The Word became flesh and blood, and moved in to the neighborhood."

"As the Father has sent Me, I also send you." Jesus sends us into the neighborhoods. He sends us to communities of need.

Communities of need are areas of our cities and towns where people are particularly vulnerable to damaging outcomes. Research tells us that multiple risk factors have a cumulative effect on well-being. One risk has a negligible effect on well-being. Two or three risks increase the chance of damaging outcomes by four. Four or more risks increase the chance of damaging outcomes by ten.

Imagine crossing a street. Little traffic means little risk. Now imagine crossing the Bruckner Expressway that I can see from the window of my apartment. A high volume of traffic means greater risk. Effective ministry works in communities of need to help individuals learn how to safely navigate in the traffic.

We can use many methods to meet these needs. They all involve being kingdom-minded—applying the upside-down principles of God's kingdom that Jesus taught and exemplified. Upside-down individuals live their lives on mission. Upside-down churches meet needs in their community. Upside-down businesses focus not just on profits but also on growing God's kingdom. Upside-down nonprofits work to provide both relief and release for their communities.

For kingdom growth, all these methods must involve a key element: planting seeds of the gospel. As we meet needs, we talk about the kingdom. Just as Jesus did, we tell people the good news while inviting them to repent and believe in Him as Savior and Lord.

In 1 Corinthians 3:6, Paul said, "I planted, Apollos watered, but God gave the growth." God grows faith. Yet Paul and Apollos had a role to play.

Consider Paul's environment during the first century. Rome was spreading its power and influence in the west. China was strengthening and expanding westward with an army sixty thousand strong. Christianity was a movement with no apparent hope of succeeding. It began with a few devotees whose leader was executed like a criminal. These followers faced ridicule from the religious, excommunication from family, murder by mobs, and persecution from their government.

Nevertheless, the church began in this environment. It didn't just add a few here and there; it boomed.

How did this happen? Jesus taught us. He told a story about a farmer who hurls seed out on the ground.

> As he was sowing, some seed fell along the path, and the birds came and ate them up. Others fell on rocky ground, where there wasn't much soil, and they sprang up quickly since the soil wasn't deep. But when the sun came up they were scorched, and since they had no root, they withered. Others fell among thorns, and the thorns came up and choked them. Still others fell on good ground and produced a crop: some 100, some 60, and some 30 times what was sown. (MATTHEW 13:4–8)

This isn't a parable that is left to us to interpret. Jesus interprets it for His disciples.

> When anyone hears the word about the kingdom and doesn't understand it, the evil one comes and snatches away what was sown in his heart. This is the one sown

along the path. And the one sown on rocky ground—this is one who hears the word and immediately receives it with joy. Yet he has no root in himself, but is short-lived. When pressure or persecution comes because of the word, immediately he stumbles. Now the one sown among the thorns—this is one who hears the word, but the worries of this age and the seduction of wealth choke the word, and it becomes unfruitful. But the one sown on the good ground—this is one who hears and under-stands the word, who does bear fruit and yields: some 100, some 60, some 30 times what was sown. (MATTHEW 13:19–23)

In this parable, only some of the seed takes root. Most of the seed seems to be squandered. Any farmer hearing this story would shake his head at the extravagance and waste of the farmer in the story. After all, seed is expensive. It makes much more sense to carefully place the seed in soil that is healthy. I guess Jesus just didn't know that much about farming.

Jesus made no mistake. Although farmers can develop a level of expertise in understanding the fertility of soil, only God knows a person's heart. I have no expertise in this arena. And yes, seed is expensive. It came at the price of Jesus' life.

Jesus is saying cast, hurl, fling, pitch, toss, throw, shoot, catapult the seed. Don't be discouraged when the results are not evident at first. It would be silly of us to plant seeds in a garden and come back the next day disappointed because they didn't grow overnight.

Paul knew his role in planting the kingdom. He said, "Remember this: The person who sows sparingly will also reap sparingly, and the person who sows generously will also reap generously" (2 Corinthians 9:6).

We sow seeds the same way Jesus did. As we meet needs, we tell people about God's kingdom, inviting them to change their thinking and put their faith in Jesus as Savior and Lord.

Remember, we are not the cause of anyone's faith; God is. The work of God in people's lives becomes evident as they profess their faith in Him.

Professors of faith are disciples. They give up their lives to live like and learn from Jesus. They learn how to do this in a local church. As they live this life, they listen to and obey Jesus, discerning His calling on their lives.

All disciples share some common callings. Every disciple is called to live in relationship with Him and live out this relationship committed to a local body of believers.

All disciples have a specific calling as well. Some are called to "go," but many are called to plant seeds of the kingdom in their own community of need.

The process starts all over.

The community is transformed one individual at a time.

God's kingdom come, His will be done on earth as it is in heaven.

CHAPTER

36 THE END

By living upside down, the upside comes down; heaven comes to earth.

Heaven is the end. That's the conclusion.

When facing the upside-down circumstances of life, darkness shrouds our minds when we lose sight of heaven, when we can't see the conclusion, when we don't know how it will end.

While taking the subway in New York City, I sometimes enjoy looking out the window from the lead car. It certainly gives me a perspective I don't have when I'm just sitting on the bench. Looking down the track, I see all kinds of things that others in the car don't. There's graffiti on the tunnel walls, rats scurrying across the track, and one time I even saw a person who subsequently got hit by the train. Believe it or not, he survived.

Looking out the front window gives the subway rider a new perspective. This perspective lends understanding to how the conductor navigates the dark tunnel. Lights shine out of the darkness of the tunnel. Sometimes these lights are red, sometimes yellow, but hopefully they are green. Much like traffic lights, green means go, yellow means caution, and red means stop—or at least that's what I've determined from my observations.

The driver of the train trusts the person who controls these lights, the dispatcher. My guess is they have never met face-to-face. Yet the conductor trusts the dispatcher's knowledge and authority. When everyone else on the train is annoyed by a train stalled in the track, the conductor trusts the red light is keeping him and everyone else from greater harm.

Navigating the struggles of our lives isn't any different. We can sit in the car wondering *why?*, or we can look at the signals. We can trust the Word of the One we have never seen and believe He is working for our good and His good.

For some reason, looking out the front of the train always makes the trip more pleasant for me. Perhaps one reason is this perspective allows me to see the lights of the station ahead. As I am leaving one station, the light of the next station is in view. I can see where we are heading.

A read through the Book of Revelation is a little like looking out the front window of the subway. We can see where we are heading. We can see how it all ends.

John was the first to see it. It's interesting to note he received this miraculous vision when he was experiencing some tough circumstances. He was exiled to the island of Patmos "because of God's word and the testimony about Jesus" (Revelation 1:9). His life had been turned upside down by the kingdom of God, and he was indeed blessed as Jesus promised!

The glorified Jesus appeared to him. Jesus was familiar, yet different. What was cloaked during His life on earth was now plainly seen. John fell at His feet. I can only imagine the comforting touch of Jesus' familiar right hand when He touched John's shoulder and said, "Don't be afraid! I am the First and the Last, and the Living One. I was dead, but look—I am alive forever and ever, and I hold the keys of death and Hades" (vv. 17–18). He is in control of sin, sickness, struggle, and death.

The next twenty-one chapters record all that John sees. It's a whirlwind of an experience. Sometimes he is seeing far off; sometimes he sees things that are near. Sometimes he is a part of the drama, and sometimes he is disconnected from it.

My understanding of this book only scratches the surface, but it keeps me coming back for more. Here is what I have learned so far.

How amazing it is to see in the throne room of God where day and night four-winged creatures, like nothing we've ever seen, sing, "Holy, holy, holy, Lord God, the Almighty, who was, who is, and who is coming" (v. 8). Reading this passage and others like it, we begin to understand that the story isn't about our good, our glory, or us. Instead, it's all about Him. Yet we are blessed because our good is wrapped up in His good.

Another passage describes crowns being cast at God's feet as the casters of those crowns say, "Our Lord and God, You are worthy to receive glory and honor and power, because You have created all things, and because of Your will they exist and were created" (Revelation 4:11).

"All things" can only mean one thing: *all* things. All the good and all the bad of my life are in the hands of a Master Gardener, Great Physician, Creator, Artist, Author who is writing the story.

This story includes great tribulation. The Book of Revelation doesn't tell the story of a struggle-free journey to the end. Rather, things lie ahead which we can only imagine—I guess we don't have to imagine, because John wrote it down for us to see. We can anticipate earthquakes, disease, meteors, darkness, hail, war, pestilence, and destruction. It's so bad that an angel is heard crying, "Woe! Woe! Woe to those who live on the earth" (8:13).

The faithful are not exempt from this tribulation but instead go through it. John sees a multitude clothed in white from every nation, tribe, people, and language. They are praising God saying, "Salvation belongs to our God, who is seated on the throne, and to the Lamb!" (7:10).

John asks who these people are. He is told:

> *These are the ones coming out of the great tribulation.*
> *They washed their robes and made them white in the*

blood of the Lamb. For this reason they are before the throne of God, and they serve Him day and night in His sanctuary. The One seated on the throne will shelter them: They will no longer hunger; they will no longer thirst; the sun will no longer strike them nor will any heat. For the Lamb who is at the center of the throne will shepherd them; He will guide them to springs of living waters, and God will wipe away every tear from their eyes. (Revelation 7:14–17)

The eternally-minded aren't exempt from tribulation, but instead go through it. They are saved from the sin, sickness, struggle, and death of life not by avoiding those things, but are saved by the One who experienced those struggles firsthand. They are saved by an Author who inserted Himself into the story, not exempting Himself from the bad things.

Those bad things are now the reason a new song is being sung in heaven: "You are worthy to take the scroll and to open its seals, because You were slaughtered, and You redeemed people for God by Your blood" (5:9).

By His blood I am redeemed. By His blood I am given my value back. By His blood I am not dust; I am gold. By His blood I am brought to a never-ending artesian well of life.

We are told in the end that every tear will be wiped away from the eyes of the ones who lived upside down through the sin, sickness, struggle, and death of their life. These people are eternally satisfied. They have joy!

Perhaps one of the greatest joys for a pale, white boy like me is I will no longer need to wear any sunscreen. "The sun will no longer strike them nor will any heat" (7:16).

This joy isn't merely something in the future. It is an already, not-yet reality.

Seven times, people are declared blessed.

1. *"The one who reads this is blessed, and those who hear the words of this prophecy and keep what is written in it are blessed, because the time is near!"* (REVELATION 1:3).

2. *"Then I heard a voice from heaven saying, 'Write: The dead who die in the Lord from now on are blessed.' 'Yes,' says the Spirit, 'let them rest from their labors, for their works follow them!'"* (14:13).

3. *"Look, I am coming like a thief. The one who is alert and remains clothed so that he may not go around naked and people see his shame is blessed"* (16:15).

4. *"Then he said to me, 'Write: Those invited to the marriage feast of the Lamb are fortunate!' He also said to me, 'These words of God are true'"* (19:9).

5. *"Blessed and holy is the one who shares in the first resurrection! The second death has no power over them, but they will be priests of God and of the Messiah, and they will reign with Him for 1,000 years"* (20:6).

6. *"Look, I am coming quickly! The one who keeps the prophetic words of this book is blessed"* (22:7).

7. *"Blessed are those who wash their robes, so that they may have the right to the tree of life and may enter the city by the gates"* (22:14).

All of these passages are in the present tense. They don't say, "Blessed will be . . ." They say, "Blessed is . . . Blessed are . . ."

Blessing and joy are already a reality for those that live each moment with the end in mind.

Yet we know something greater is yet to come.

At the end of the Book of Revelation, we see the dawning of this new world. But first, there is a funeral. It's a funeral for sin, sickness, struggle, and death. "Death and Hades were thrown into the lake of fire" (20:14).

Then we see a new creation where "death will no longer exist; grief, crying, and pain will exist no longer, because the previous things have passed away" (21:4).

This new creation is a city. This city is described in 21–22. I have been reminded by my mentor that we may have begun in a garden but we all have an urban future. He has made the following observations about this city:

- It's safe, with huge walls; yet there is freedom. The gates are always open.

- People walk the gold streets where there is no more poverty or pain.

- A river runs through the city, just like in Eden. On both sides of this river is a tree. The multifaceted fruit of this tree is life and the healing of the nations. Racism is no more.

- We will have no more darkness or confusion; God is the light. We are blessed by His presence. His kingdom has come, His will done.

This is a city where I want to live. The sin, sickness, struggle, and death of my life have made me hungry for this place. I thank God for these things because they have not only opened my eyes to the eternal reality but have helped me smash my idols, find cancerous joy, grow through struggle, and die to self. God has changed the way I think. He has healed me physically and spiritually. He has given me new perspectives. He has given me deeper understanding.

In the end, my story isn't all that consequential. The only story that will matter is the one "written in the Lamb's book of life" (Revelation 21:27).

Meanwhile, as CS Lewis described in his last installment of *The Chronicles of Narnia*, my experiences in this world—all the sin, sickness, struggle, and death of this life, as well as all the happiness, satisfaction, and joy—are merely the "beginning of the real story. . . . [Just] the cover and title page" (*The Last Battle*).

We can only imagine "Chapter One of the Great Story which no one on earth has read: which goes on forever: in which every chapter is better than the one before" (*The Last Battle*).

Yes, there are moments in the story that seem upside down. However, the only way I have learned to see right-side up is by being turned upside down. In each of those circumstances God was doing more than I could dare ask, hope or imagine.

AUGUST 18, 2011

"Dad is in a mood. I still get so frustrated with him. It is hard to ignore. I don't know what to do to make the situation better."

I never dared to consider the struggles I experienced in my relationship with my father were shaping me into the man I would become. I now have a different perspective.

DECEMBER 19, 2011

"Andrew, something happened. . . . Your dad passed away."

There was a lot I didn't understand. However through his death, I began to understand the certainty of hope that sprouts from the root of faith.

AUGUST 27, 2012

"We found a mass. It looks like testicular cancer."

I never asked God to heal my soul. I didn't know I needed it. However, through cancer, the Great Physician brought more than just physical healing.

JULY 27, 2014

"For 16 years of my life, I have been disobedient. I need to be right before God and before my church. I need to be baptized."

I went from being a master of religion, concerned about what others thought, to being obedient to Jesus. I only cared what He thought!

God has used the upside-down circumstances of life to give me joy, and He is working to make my joy complete!

By being turned upside down the upside has come down.

RESOURCES FOR UPSIDE-DOWN LIVING!

To learn more about this series, visit NewHopePublishers.com.

Upside-Down Leadership
Rethinking Influence and Success
TAYLOR FIELD

ISBN-13: 978-1-59669-342-5
N124147 $14.99

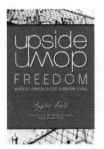

Upside-Down Freedom
Inverted Principles for Christian Living
TAYLOR FIELD

ISBN-13: 978-1-59669-376-0
N134117 $14.99

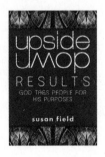

Upside-Down Results
God Tags People for His Purposes
SUSAN FIELD

ISBN-13: 978-1-59669-404-0
N144110 $14.99

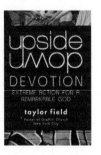

Upside-Down Devotion
Extreme Action for a Remarkable God
TAYLOR FIELD

ISBN 13: 978-1-59669-405-7
N144111 $14.99

Available in bookstores everywhere.

WorldCrafts™ artisan partner Graffiti 2 Works in the South Bronx of New York coaches adults in developing the physical, mental, emotional, social, and spiritual skills necessary to become the best he or she is capable of becoming. Program components include life skills, spirtual direction, mentoring, educational skills, career connections, and job incentive. Currently the group has four artisans who are taking classes with the goal of receiving their GED. These artisans range from 18 to 22 years old and have all lived in the South Bronx their entire life. Learning sewing skills and selling products not only provides them with a little money in their pockets, but it also builds their self-esteem and helps give them practical knowledge for the future.

WORLDCRAFTS℠

Committed. Holistic. Fair Trade.

WorldCrafts.org 1-800-968-7301